40

GREAT RAIL-TRAILS

in the Mid-Atlantic

by Karen-Lee Ryan

♦♦♦

RAILS-TO-TRAILS CONSERVANCY
SATURN CORPORATION

Cover and interior design: Cutting Edge Graphics

Maps by Mark A. Wood

✪ Printed on recycled paper

ISBN 0-925794-10-4

Manufactured in the United States of America

10 9 8 7 6 5 4 3 2 1

Acknowledgements

This book resulted from the extraordinary partnership between Rails-to-Trails Conservancy, Saturn Corporation, Hearst Magazines and Hal Riney & Partners. I am grateful to many people who made the relationship possible.

From Saturn, thanks to Don Hudler, Vice President, Sales/Marketing/Service; Steve Shannon, Director of Consumer Marketing; Dianne A. Romanelli, Advertising Coordinator; and Mary Wernette, National Advertising Manager.

From Hearst, thanks to Mark E. Goldschmidt, Vice President Marketing and Sales; Bridget Zukas, *Cosmopolitan* Detroit Manager and Janine Walters, *Cosmopolitan* San Francisco Manager.

From Hal Riney and Partners, thanks to Ellen Kiyomizu, Vice President, Associate Media Director; Nina Ward, Account Executive; Elisha Moore, Assistant Account Executive; and Doris Mitsch, Senior Writer.

Diane Romanelli of Saturn and Mark Goldschmidt of Hearst Magazines were the lead corporate contacts and deserve special recognition for supporting the project and efficiently overseeing it.

Thanks also go to Lisa McGimsey White and Bruce E. White of White & White, Inc. for helping us launch the partnership.

I also need to recognize several individuals for their involvement with the project.

Thanks to RTC President David Burwell for providing me the opportunity to write this book and for allowing me to take time away from the office to do the necessary on-site trail research.

Sharon Benjamin, Rails-to-Trails Conservancy's Vice President for Marketing, continually advanced the relationship with Saturn and Hearst by maintaining open communication. Her unwavering support for the book, coupled with her superior management skills, kept me motivated throughout the entire project.

Special thanks to two people without whose help this book may never have been finished: Nicole Cox and April Moore. Nicole

diligently fact-checked the book under rigorous deadlines—and offered a supporting smile every step of the way. April conducted a thorough copyedit of the entire manuscript, while providing moral support via phone and fax practically on a daily basis.

Mark Wood may be the only other person who knows what it took to put this book together, as he was involved every step of the way. In addition to accompanying me on several trail tours, he dedicated an incredible number of hours to creating all the maps in the book. His biggest contribution, however, was his constant encouragement of my involvement with the project.

Sally James of Cutting Edge Graphics used her creative talents to design the book's cover and interior pages. She also carefully labeled all the maps. Her calming personality kept me focused on each step of the production process, while her clever design solutions kept the project on deadline.

I also want to express my appreciation to Seneca Murley, Program Assistant of Rails-to-Trails Conservancy's Ohio Chapter, and Tom Sexton, Chapter Coordinator of Rails-to-Trails Conservancy's Pennsylvania Chapter. Both took time from their busy schedules to join me in exploring many trails. Seneca also wrote the text for the Olentangy-Scioto Bikeway, while Tom contributed the Stony Valley Railroad Grade description.

Thanks also to several individuals who contributed to the book: Lynn Hartman and Frank Proud of the West Virginia Rails-to-Trails Council for their work on the Greenbrier River Trail and the West Fork Trail; J. Wandres of New Jersey for his work on the Henry Hudson Trail; Robert Barth of the Paulinskill Valley Trail Committee for work on the Paulinskill Valley Trail; and Brian Schmult of New Jersey Rail Trails for coordinating the New Jersey information.

Several trail volunteers deserve acknowledgment for their hospitality in leading me on tours of their trails: Laurie and Jim LaFontaine, Ghost Town Trail; David Howes, Allegheny River Trail; and Shawn Richardson, Thomas J. Evans Bikeway.

Finally, I would like to thank all the trail managers in the book for answering questions and providing additional information for the wonderful rail-trails selected for this book.

Karen-Lee Ryan
April, 1995

Foreword

By now, you've probably noticed the Saturn name on the cover of this book. And, if you have, you may be asking a very logical question: why would a car company want to sponsor a guide to a network of "roads" where you can't even drive?

Well, at Saturn, we feel very lucky to live and work in such a beautiful country. And, while we certainly want you to enjoy our cars, we also want you to be able to leave them in the garage now and then.

Which brings us to the subject of this book.

Before cars became our main mode of transportation, cities, towns, parks and forests all across America were connected by the most expansive railway system in the world. Nowadays, thousands of miles of rail corridors are abandoned every year—thousands of miles that pass through some of America's most amazing scenery and interesting places to visit. Fortunately, many of these empty railroad corridors are being converted to a different kind of transportation system.

Rail-trails are not only a beautiful way of preserving an important part of our country's history, they're also ideal for all kinds of sporting and outdoor activities, from walking to bicycling to cross-country skiing.

So we hope you'll take the time to explore a few of the rail-trails in this book—whether it's just for a little fresh air and exercise, to do some sightseeing or simply to get from point A to point B without using a drop of gasoline.

Who knows? Maybe you'll even be inspired to help preserve more rail-trails—in which case, Rails-to-Trails Conservancy would be delighted to hear from you.

In the meantime, let's hit the trail.

From the Saturn Team

Introduction

Welcome to an American adventure! Within these pages, you will find 40 unique experiences on America's fastest growing network of pathways to adventure: rail-trails.

Across the country, thousands of miles of former railroad corridors have been converted to trails for recreation, transportation and open space preservation. Whether you are a bicyclist, a walker, an equestrian, a wheelchair user, a cross-country skier, an in-line skater or an outdoor enthusiast, rail-trails are for you!

Rail-trails traverse every conceivable environment from urban to suburban to rural, passing through farmland, river valleys, wetlands, residential areas, forests and lake shores. In metropolitan areas, rail-trails serve as linear parks that provide a respite from the hustle and bustle of everyday life. In rural areas, they run through some of the most scenic and pristine landscapes in America.

The Mid-Atlantic region—Pennsylvania, New Jersey, Maryland, Virginia, West Virginia and Ohio—plays a key role in the rails-to-trails movement.

Pennsylvania is one of the nation's top rail-trail states. It has 54 rail-trails totaling nearly 550 miles and more rail-trail projects than any other state. Ohio boasts 21 trails totaling 240 miles, and West Virginia is close behind with 12 trails totaling nearly 200 miles. New Jersey and Virginia each offer about 150 miles of trails and Maryland has developed nearly 50 miles. (Delaware is one of only two states in the nation without a rail-trail, although several projects are underway.)

The trails selected for *40 Great Rail-Trails in the Mid-Atlantic* offer surprising diversity and intriguing experiences for any trail user. New and exciting places await you on these trails—places where you can pass through brick-lined tunnels that extend more than 2,000 feet, explore ghost towns that thrived during the coal-mining boom, travel along North America's oldest river, venture through the valley where oil was first discovered and drilled, view native

American burial mounds, discover the area that inspired the world's first roller coaster, or visit a historical museum housed in an old railroad depot. These 40 great rail-trails will lead you to these places and many more.

History of the Rail-Trail Movement

In 1916, the United States was home to the world's most extensive railroad network, with virtually every community connected together by routes of steel. At the pinnacle of the railroading era, nearly 300,000 miles of track spanned the nation—a network six times larger than today's interstate highway system.

Now, *less than half* of that original railroad network exists. Cars, trucks, buses and airplanes have led to the rapid decline of the railroad industry, which continues to abandon more than 2,000 miles of track every year.

The concept of preserving these valuable corridors and converting them into multi-use public trails began in the Midwest, where railroad abandonments were most widespread. Once the tracks came out, people naturally started using the corridors for walking and hiking while exploring railroad relics ranging from train stations and mills to bridges and tunnels.

While many people agreed with this great new concept, the reality of actually converting abandoned rail lines into public trails was a much greater challenge. From the late 1960s until the early 1980s, many rail-trail efforts failed as corridors were lost to development, sold to the highest bidder or broken into many pieces.

In 1983, Congress enacted an amendment to the National Trails System Act directing the Interstate Commerce Commission to allow about-to-be abandoned railroad lines to be "railbanked," or set aside for future transportation use while being used as trails in the interim. In essence, this law preempts rail corridor abandonment, keeping the corridors intact for trail use and any possible future railroad uses.

This powerful new piece of legislation made it easier for agencies and organizations to acquire rail corridors for trails, but many projects still failed because of short deadlines, lack of information and local opposition to trails.

In 1986, Rails-to-Trails Conservancy (RTC) formed to provide a

national voice for the creation of rail-trails. RTC quickly developed a strategy to preserve the largest amount of rail corridor in the shortest period of time: a national advocacy program to defend the new railbanking law in the courts and in Congress, coupled with a direct project assistance program to help public agencies and local rail-trail groups overcome the challenges of converting a rail into a trail.

The strategy is working! In 1986, RTC knew of only 75 rail-trails and 90 projects in the works. Today, there are more than 660 rail-trails and an additional 900 projects underway. The Rails-to-Trails Conservancy vision of creating an interconnected network of trails across the country is becoming a reality.

The thriving rails-to-trails movement has created more than 7,400 miles of public trails for a wide range of users. And, in 1993, these rail-trails were used more than 86 million times. People all across the country are now realizing the incredible benefits of rail-trails.

Benefits of Rail-Trails

Rail-trails are flat or have gentle grades, making them perfect for multiple users, ranging from walkers and bicyclists to in-line skaters and people with disabilities. In snowy climates, they are perfect for cross-country skiing, snowmobiling and other snow activities. And, because of their length, they offer numerous access points.

In urban areas, rail-trails act as linear greenways through developed areas, efficiently providing much-needed recreation space while also serving as utilitarian transportation corridors. They link neighborhoods and workplaces and connect congested areas to open spaces. In many cities and suburbs, rail-trails are used for commuting to work, school and shopping.

In rural ares, rail-trails can provide a significant stimulus to local economies. People who use trails often spend money on food, beverages, camping, hotels, bed-and-breakfasts, bicycle rentals, souvenirs and other items. Studies have shown that trail users have generated as much as $1.25 million annually for the towns through which a trail passes.

Rail-trails preserve historic structures, such as train stations, bridges, tunnels, mills, factories and canals. These structures preserve an important piece of history and enhance the trail experience.

Wildlife viewing also enhances the trail experience, and rail-trails are home to birds, plants, wetlands and a variety of small and large mammals. Many rail-trails serve as conservation corridors, and, in some cases, protect endangered species.

Recreation, transportation, historic preservation, economic revitalization, open space conservation and wildlife preservation— these are just some of the many benefits of rail-trails and the reasons why people love them.

How to Get Involved

If you enjoy rail-trails, join the movement to save abandoned rail corridors and to create more trails across the country. Donating even a small amount of your time can help get more trails on the ground.

◆ If you only have an hour, write a letter to your city, county or state elected official in favor of pro rail-trail legislation. You could also write a letter to the editor of your local newspaper praising a trail or trail project. Or, you could attend a public hearing to voice your support for a local trail, or send a letter to a friend sharing the special qualities of rail-trails.

◆ If you have a day, volunteer to plant flowers or trees along an existing trail or spend several hours helping out with a cleanup on a nearby rail-trail project. Or, lead a hike along an abandoned corridor with your friends.

◆ If you have several hours a month, become an active member in a trail effort in your area. Many groups host trail events, undertake fundraising campaigns, publish brochures and newsletters and carry out other activities to promote a trail or project. Virtually all of these efforts are completed by volunteers, and they are always looking for another helping hand.

Whatever your time allows, get involved! The success of a community's rail-trail depends upon the level of citizen participation. Rails-to-Trails Conservancy can put you in touch with a local group in your area. And, if you want to keep up on and support the movement nationally, join Rails-to-Trails Conservancy. You will get discounts on all RTC merchandise, and you will be supporting the largest national trails organization in the United States. To become a member, use the order form at the back of this book.

How to Use Rail-Trails

By design, rail-trails accommodate a variety of trail users. While this is generally one of the many benefits of rail-trails, it also can lead to occasional conflicts among trail users. Everyone should take responsibility to ensure trail safety by following a few simple trail etiquette guidelines.

One of the most basic etiquette rules is, "Wheels yield to heels." The figure below indicates the correct protocol for yielding right-of-way. Bicyclists (and in-line skaters) yield to other users; pedestrians yield to equestrians.

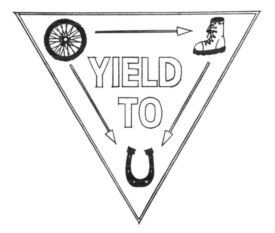

Generally, this means that you need to warn users (to whom you are yielding) of your presence. If, as a bicyclist, you fail to warn a walker that you are about to pass, the walker could step in front you, causing an accident that could have been prevented. Similarly, it is best to slow down and warn an equestrian of your presence. A horse can be startled by a bicycle, so make verbal contact with the rider and be sure it is safe to pass.

Here are some other guidelines you should follow to promote trail safety:

- ◆ Obey all trail-use rules posted at trailheads.
- ◆ Stay to the right except when passing
- ◆ Pass slower traffic on their left; yield to oncoming traffic when passing.
- ◆ Give a clear warning signal when passing; for example, call out, "Passing on your left."
- ◆ Always look ahead and behind when passing.
- ◆ Travel at a reasonable speed.
- ◆ Keep pets on a leash.
- ◆ Do not trespass on private property.
- ◆ Move off the trail surface when stopped to allow others to pass.
- ◆ Yield to other trail users when entering and crossing the trail.
- ◆ Do not disturb any wildlife.

How to Use This Book

At the beginning of each state, you will find a map showing the general location of each rail-trail listed in that state. The text description of every rail-trail begins with the following information:

Trail Name: The official name of the rail-trail is stated here.

Endpoints: This heading lists the endpoints for the entire trail, usually identified by a municipality or a nearby geographical point.

Location: The county or counties through which the trail passes are stated here.

Length: This indicates the length of the trail, including how many miles currently are open, and for those trails that are built partially on abandoned corridors, the number of miles actually on the rail line.

Surface: The materials that make up the surface of the rail-trail vary from trail to trail, and this heading describes each trail's surface, which ranges from asphalt and crushed stone to the significantly more rugged original railroad ballast.

Contact: The name, address and telephone number of each trail's manager are listed here. The selected contacts generally are responsible for managing the trail and can provide additional information about the trail and its condition.

Legend

In addition, every trail has a series of icons depicting uses allowed on the trail.

 walking, hiking, running

 in-line skating and roller-skating

 bicycling

 fishing access

 mountain bikes recommended

 cross-country skiing

horseback riding

 snowmobiling

 wheelchair access

Uses permitted on individual trails are based on trail surfaces and are determined solely by trail managers. Rails-to-Trails Conservancy has no control over which uses are permitted and prohibited.

Wheelchair access is indicated for hard-surface trails. All trails that allow bicycling also allow mountain bicycling, but only on the trail surface—not in surrounding open areas. Trails that only list the mountain bicycling symbol have rougher terrains that are not suitable for road bikes

Map Legend

●	Trail endpoints	— — —	County borders
▬	Rail-Trail	— — —	State borders
ℙ	Parking	(95)	Interstate highway
◆	Point of interest	(301)	U.S. highway
·········	Active railroad track	(213)	State Route
—··—··—	Federal park or forest boundary		

Rail-Trail Safety

The author of this book has made every effort to ensure the accuracy of the information included here, however trails and their conditions can change at any time. It is your responsibility to ensure your own safety and exercise caution while using rail-trails. This includes knowing the limits of your own abilities and wearing a helmet when bicycling.

If you find inaccurate information or substantially different conditions, please send a letter detailing your findings to: Publications Department, Rails-to-Trails Conservancy, 1400 Sixteenth Street, NW, Washington, DC 20036.

An Introduction to Rail-Trails in Pennsylvania

With nearly 60 rail-trails totaling almost 700 miles, Pennsylvania is among the top states with trails created from abandoned railroad corridors. This achievement provides safe and scenic places for individuals and families to enjoy, while preserving an important piece of Pennsylvania's heritage.

The railroad industry played a critical role in developing the Keystone State, which was once home to nearly 12,000 miles of railroad tracks. Today, less than half remain active. Fortunately, people throughout the state took a lead role to preserve key corridors as trails.

By 1988, the Pennsylvania Chapter of Rails-to-Trails Conservancy had been created to help promote rail-trails throughout the state. With a two-person office based in Harrisburg, the Pennsylvania Chapter works to get more rail-trails on the ground by providing technical assistance to agencies and local rail-trail groups, by working with elected officials, and by publicizing the rail-trail movement throughout the state.

All of the hard work is paying off, as new trails open and others are extended. And, an incredible number of interconnected networks are forming throughout the state. In western Pennsylvania, trail advocates—working with various agencies—have developed plans to create a 315-mile interconnected network of trails. By the year 2000, downtown Pittsburgh could connect to downtown Washington, D.C. using a vast system of rail-trails and the C&O Canal National Historical Park. In the future, the system could extend all the way to Erie in the state's northwest corner.

This book offers you a glimpse of these forming networks, while introducing you to the other exceptional trails throughout the state. From Philadelphia to Pittsburgh and from Jim Thorpe to Oil City, the trails chosen for this book highlight Pennsylvania's heritage and diversity.

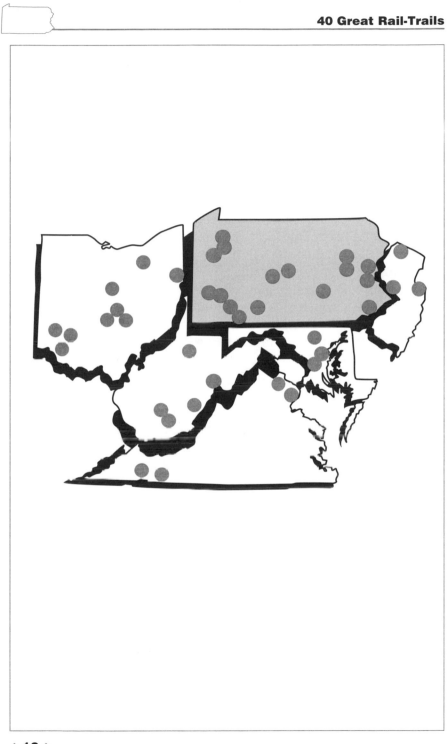

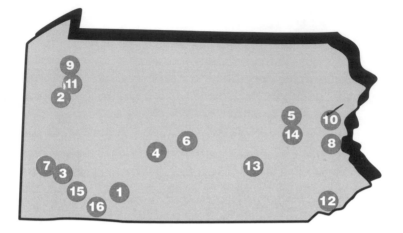

PENNSYLVANIA'S GREAT RAIL-TRAILS

1. Allegheny Highlands Trail
2. Allegheny River Trail
3. Arrowhead Trail
4. Ghost Town Trail
5. Lehigh Gorge State Park *great trail (2 hr. drive) 8/01*
6. Lower Trail
7. Montour Trail
8. National Trails Towpath Bike Trail of Palmer and Bethlehem Townships
9. Oil Creek State Park
10. Plainfield Township Trail *great trail 8/01 (lots of steps at gates because they are not well designed)*
11. Samuel Justus Recreational Trail
12. Schuylkill River Trail
13. Stony Valley Railroad Grade
14. Switchback Railroad Trail
15. Youghiogheny River Trail (North)
16. Youghiogheny River Trail (South)

The Allegheny Highlands Trail offers many excellent fishing spots.

Allegheny Highlands Trail

Endpoints: Garrett to Markleton

Location: Somerset County

Length: 14 miles (will be 60 miles when completed)

Surface: hard-packed crushed limestone

Uses: 🚶 🚲 ♿ 🎣 ⛷️

Contact: Hank Parke
Somerset County Rails-to-Trails Association
829 North Center Avenue
Somerset, PA 15501
814-445-6431

◆◆◆

A critical piece of the proposed Pittsburgh to Washington multi-use trail, the Allegheny Highlands Trail is the missing link that will connect the 75-mile Youghiogheny River Trail network with the 180-mile towpath of the C&O Canal National Historical Park. When completed, this trail will extend from Confluence, Pennsylvania, to Cumberland, Maryland.

The Allegheny Highlands Trail got its start as the Connellsville Extension of the Western Maryland Railroad, which opened in 1912. Located along the Casselman River, this line was part of a through-freight route between New York and Chicago. As rail usage declined over the years, this corridor became unnecessary, and it was finally abandoned in 1975. The county opened the first seven miles of trail in the spring of 1993 and another seven in the summer of 1994.

The trail's current southeastern terminus is located in the village of Garrett. Surrounded by coal mines in the late 1800s, the town offered three stores, two blacksmith shops, a boarding house

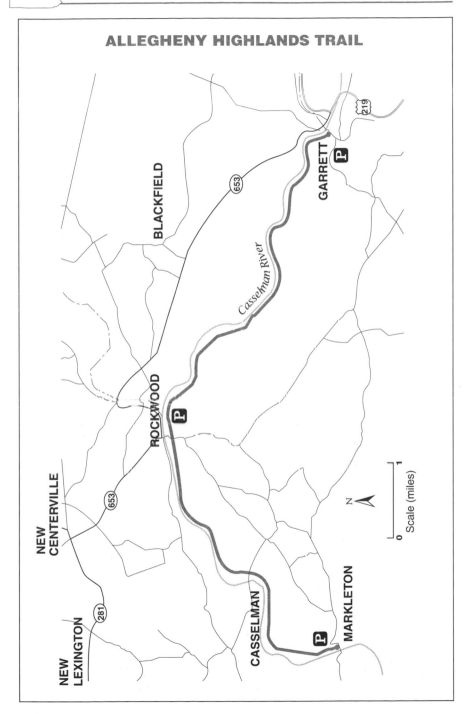

ALLEGHENY HIGHLANDS TRAIL

and a saw mill. Today, several historic buildings remain and the population is barely 500 people. Just outside Garrett is Mount Davis, the highest point in Pennsylvania at 3,213 feet. Therefore, the trail is on a slight decline all the way to Markleton.

To reach the Garrett trailhead, take State Route 653 west from U.S. Route 219. Shortly, you will take a left onto Berlin Street, and cross over the Casselman River. Take a right onto Water Works Street and into the trail parking lot, where a portable toilet is located.

Eventually, the trail will extend another 16.5 miles to the Maryland border and then into Cumberland. The 10 miles south of Garrett include the 3,500-foot Savage Tunnel and the 1,900 foot-long Salisbury Viaduct Bridge. The segment that will link to Confluence includes the 850-foot Pinkerton Tunnel. The entire "missing link" is slated for completion by 1999.

You will pass through two gates as you make your way onto the trail, and in less than a mile, you will pass mile marker 17. The management has cleverly placed their mile markers to indicate the distance from the Maryland border.

As soon as you get onto the trail, you enter a peaceful world, with the Casselman River lightly rippling off to your right.

Tom Sexton

Wildflowers add a fragrant dimension to the Allegheny Highlands Trail during the spring and summer months.

Rhododendrons and ferns line the trail's left side, which is home to a variety of wildlife, including white-tailed deer, grouse and wild turkey. If you are lucky, you might also catch a glimpse of a red-tailed hawk.

Beyond mile marker 18, a wall of chiseled rocks appears on the left. Soon, you will see a gate on the river side of the trail, which signals a series of limestone caves on the opposite bank. If you take a look across the river and above the active railroad tracks, you can see several openings in the limestone wall.

For the next few miles, the trail remains quite pristine and remote with few changes along the way. The dense woods surrounding you include hemlocks, oaks, maples, beeches and dogwoods. Near mile marker 22, a small waterfall often trickles from the rocky banks that occasionally creep out of the woods.

Within a half-mile you will pass by a small power sub-station after a few power lines make an abrupt—and brief—appearance along the trail. Then, the views begin to open up, and you will see an old coal-waste pile to remind you of the route's origins. Just before entering Rockwood, the intriguing limestone shelves reappear on the left side.

You will make an at-grade crossing at State Route 653, which will lead you into a large trail parking lot. A gas station/convenience store, with refreshments and a public phone, is near the parking lot. The town of Rockwood, where you can find a couple of restaurants and a hardware store, is downhill to the right on the opposite bank of the Casselman River.

Within about a half-mile, you will pass mile marker 24. Many wildflowers—black eyed-susans, bee balm, violets and daisies—dot the route over the next few miles. In the summer, they produce a delightful, sweet aroma. As you approach mile marker 27, water often seeps and trickles over the rock ledges along the trail's left side. The river, meanwhile, darts in and out of view.

As you approach mile marker 29, you will view the Markleton parking lot in the distance. Just before you reach the gate leading to the lot, you will see an old mine shaft on the trail's right side. Portable toilets are located in the parking lot.

Within a couple of years, the Allegheny Highlands Trail will continue 12 miles southwest to Confluence, where it will meet up with the southern section of the Youghiogheny River Trail (see page 95).

Allegheny River Trail

Endpoints: Franklin to Brandon

Location: Venango County

Length: 15 miles

Surface: 5 miles of asphalt beginning in Franklin and 10 miles of large, chunky original ballast

Uses:

 on first five miles

Contact: Franklin Area Chamber of Commerce
1256 Liberty Street, Suite 2
Franklin, PA 16323
814-432-5823

◆◆◆

Located about two hours from Pittsburgh, Cleveland and Buffalo, the Allegheny River Trail seems destined to attract thousands of bicyclists from Pennsylvania, Ohio and New York. And when this river's edge trail is fully developed and linked to other trail corridors in Western Pennsylvania, it may well attract trail users from just about any state. Quite a feat, given that the Allegheny River Trail project is run entirely by volunteers.

The Allegheny River Trail is the newest section of what will eventually become a 170 mile-long trail along one of Pennsylvania's major rivers. It is also a major segment of the Pittsburgh to Erie trail route, which will someday connect to the Pittsburgh to Washington, D.C. trail.

The trailhead is located just east of Franklin in a large parking lot alongside U.S Route 322. This lot joins the Allegheny River Trail's

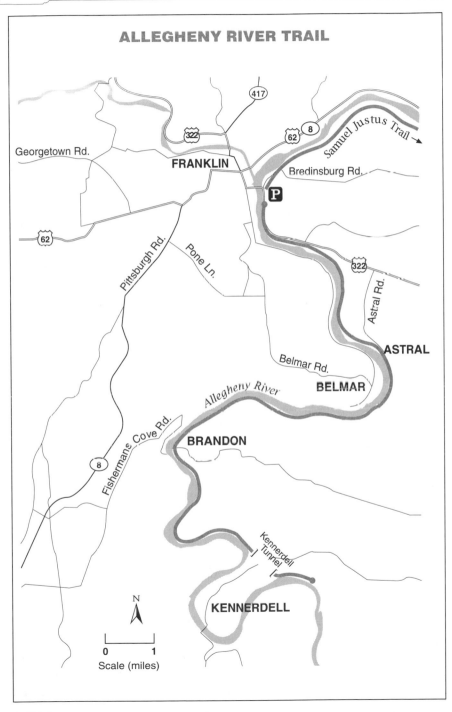

ALLEGHENY RIVER TRAIL

417

322

62 8

Samuel Justus Trail →

Georgetown Rd.

FRANKLIN

Bredinsburg Rd.

P

62

Pittsburgh Rd.

Pone Ln.

322

Astral Rd.

ASTRAL

Belmar Rd.

Allegheny River

BELMAR

Fishermans Cove Rd.

8

BRANDON

Kennerdell Tunnel

N

KENNERDELL

0   1
Scale (miles)

Karen-Lee Ryan

The serene Allegheny River makes an excellent backdrop for this 15-mile trail.

northern endpoint with the southern endpoint of the Samuel Justus Trail (see page 65). While the trails have different ownership and management, they take their origins from the same former railroad corridor.

The corridor was operated most recently by Conrail, which abandoned the line in 1984 as use diminished. In 1991, PG&E-Bechtel Generating Company donated the 15-mile segment to the volunteer-run Allegheny Valley Trails Association.

In the summer of 1994, the first five miles were surfaced with macadam (a course asphalt), and a couple of bridges were decked. Few additional improvements have been made, but it's obvious that the trail corridor has great potential. The trail starts out parallel-ing U.S. Route 322. Within 1.5 miles, a gradual hill rises between the trail and the road, leaving the trail quietly tucked along the edge of the Allegheny River. At about the same time, views of the expansive river start getting clearer.

Near mile marker two, you will see a series of islands on the Allegheny River. They are federally-designated wilderness areas and are home to many species of wildlife. Primitive camping, accessed

by canoe, is allowed on the islands. Primitive camping is also allowed along the trail, and designated campsites are planned as part of future development. The first site, with a fire ring and a couple of picnic tables, was recently completed just prior to mile four.

A variety of wildlife, including deer and beaver, live in the trail's vicinity. And the area is an excellent location for bird-watching, especially in late spring. Warblers, ospreys and owls can often be viewed from the trail.

Soon after mile marker four, you will see a long bridge span ahead of you that was part of the former Clarion Secondary rail line. Recently purchased for development into a trail, this line runs 40 miles between the Ohio border and the Allegheny River. It will be another key link in the extensive Western Pennsylvania trail network.

You actually reach the Clarion Secondary bridge just beyond mile marker five, where it crosses over the Allegheny River Trail near the Belmar Bridge. This junction is the end of the developed portion of the Allegheny River Trail. The Belmar bridge has not yet been decked for trail use, so if you opt to proceed on the undeveloped portion of trail, use extreme caution.

If you do continue, crossing under the Clarion Secondary bridge, you will quickly find that the surface is suitable only for durable mountain bikes or sturdy hiking boots. The large, chunky rocks were the original railroad ballast on which the tracks and ties were laid. It can be a bone-jarring ride, although this section of trail could be under development as early as summer 1995.

If you can handle the surface for about 10 miles, you will be rewarded with the Kennerdell Tunnel, a magnificent 3,800-foot long tunnel. If you plan to travel the distance, be sure to bring a flashlight. Most people end their journey just beyond the tunnel, although the undeveloped corridor continues through Clarion County and into Armstrong County. Someday, the entire corridor will be one of the nation's longest, continuous rail-trails.

Arrowhead Trail

Endpoints: Town of McMurray

Location: Washington County

Length: 4 miles (will be 6 miles when complete)

Surface: 3.5 miles of asphalt;
0.5 mile of original ballast

Uses: 🛼 🚲 ♿ 👟 ⛷️

🚲 (on 0.5-mile section)

Contact: Joanne Nelson, Director
Peters Township Department of Parks and
Recreation
610 East McMurray Road
McMurray, PA 15317
412-942-5000

◆◆◆

O pened in 1985, the Arrowhead Trail is the pioneer in the future 55-mile Montour Trail. In fact, the Arrowhead Trail was built long before the idea of developing the entire Montour Trail had even been conceived. The Arrowhead's standard of excellence, coupled with its overwhelming popularity, have set the stage for a top-notch trail that will skirt Pittsburgh's western and southern suburbs.

The Montour Railroad, which originally formed a semi-circle around the western edge of Pittsburgh, was built in 1877 to carry coal to local coke ovens. Despite the coal industry's decline, the Pittsburgh and Lake Erie Railroad purchased the line in 1975 , and then abandoned this section of track in 1980. Peters Township

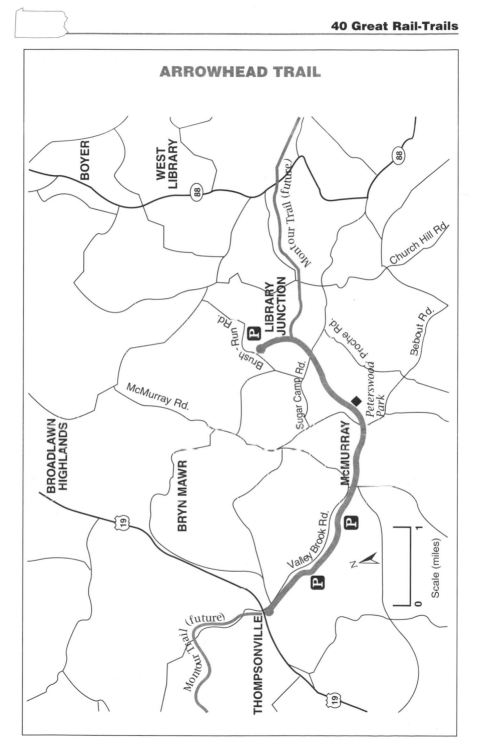

ARROWHEAD TRAIL

purchased the right of way, and an additional 100 acres of land, and opened the Arrowhead Trail in 1985. Four years later, the Montour Trail Council formed to convert the entire 55-mile corridor into a multi-use trail. The rest of the Montour Trail is described beginning on page 44.

To reach the Arrowhead Trail's western endpoint, near Thompsonville, take Valley Brook Road east from U.S. Route 19 and travel about one mile to the signed trail parking lot on the right side. On a typical summer week night this lot can get quite crowded, as the trail receives heavy local use. This parking lot is also home to a wildflower area planted by the Giant Oaks Garden Club.

You begin the paved trail after crossing over the parking lot on a bridge. You can go the opposite direction from the bridge on a gravel surface for about a half-mile if you have a mountain bike or are traveling on foot. This short stretch will be paved in 1996.

As you begin the paved section of trail, you will travel basically parallel to Valley Brook Road. Within a mile, you will cross over a bridge and pass by an additional parking area. From here, you will see a hike and bike shop and several other businesses. The trail

Karen-Lee Ryan

Families enjoy the Arrowhead Trail.

(as with other sections of the Montour Trail) remains elevated above street level, with good views to the surrounding terrain.

Less than two miles from the start of the trail, you will see a sign for Peterswood Park. This 86-acre community park includes baseball fields, picnic shelters an outdoor concert stage, restrooms and telephones. In another half-mile, you will pass a large, private horse farm off to the right side. The extensive fencing throughout the farm can make interesting photographs.

Beyond this point, the trail continues its suburban tone with several new homes built to the left of the trail. Meanwhile, woods envelop the right side. Soon the trail will rise up a short, relatively steep hill to the eastern endpoint, where you will find a large parking area located off of Brush Run Road.

Since its opening nearly 10 years ago, the Arrowhead Trail has received several awards, including an Excellence in Design Award from the Pennsylvania Department of Transportation and a conservation award for the wildflower plantings at the trail's western end. In addition, 500 trees been planted at intervals along this attractive and well-used trail.

Ghost Town Trail

Endpoints: Nanty Glo to Dilltown
with a spur to White Mill Station

Location: Cambria and Indiana Counties

Length: 15.5 miles; will be 16 miles when completed

Surface: hard-packed crushed limestone

Uses: 🚶 🚲 ♿ 🎿

🏇 by permit only

Contact: Ed Patterson
Indiana County Parks
RD 2, Box 157-J
Indiana, PA 15701
412-463-8636

◆◆◆

Traveling along the Ghost Town Trail, you might wonder where it got its name. Unless you pay close attention, you might miss the few remaining foundations along a route that once cut through several towns, including two thriving coal-mining towns that played a key role in Pennsylvania's industrial heritage. While the towns were disbanded in the 1930s, the Ghost Town Trail is keeping their spirit alive.

The route's history as a rail line began in 1903 when the Ebensburg and Back Lick Railroad opened the line. Over the years it serviced several coal mines, a nearby lumber town and three iron furnaces in the region. A flood in 1977 put the railroad out of business after 11 inches of rain fell in one night. The Conrail-owned corridor was completely wiped out.

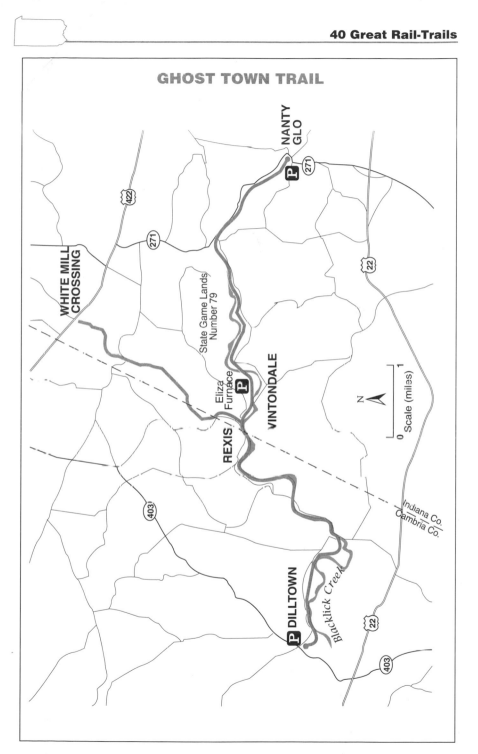

GHOST TOWN TRAIL

NANTY GLO

271

422

271

WHITE MILL CROSSING

State Game Lands Number 79

22

VINTONDALE

Eliza Furnace

REXIS

N

Scale (miles)
0   1

403

Indiana Co.
Cambria Co.

DILLTOWN

Blacklick Creek

22

403

Crossing Backlick Creek near the mid-point of the Ghost Town Trail.

In 1991 the Kovalchick Salvage Company gave new life to the corridor, donating it to Cambria and Indiana Counties. Active volunteers promoted the rail-trail project for several years, and the first 12 miles officially opened in October 1994.

To get to Nanty Glo, the trail's eastern terminus, take State Route 271 north from U.S. Route 22 and proceed 1.3 miles to the Nanty Glo Fire Department (Station 43) on the left side. The trail begins at the far end of the parking lot behind the Fire Station.

From Nanty Glo, which is a Welsh name for "valley of coal," the South Branch of Backlick Creek follows the trail's left side, and woods line the right side. Unfortunately, recent logging activity has cleared some of the more heavily wooded areas along the trail's first mile. Just beyond mile marker 2, you will cross a paved road at-grade, and then you will be entering State Game Lands 79. Hunting is allowed during much of the year, although not on Sundays.

Soon you will cross the creek on a short bridge span, and by mile 2.5, a steep, rocky outcropping towers above the trail's left side. If you look closely, you can see what looks like rust seeping from the rock. Known as coal seams, these led early industrial entrepreneurs on a fruitful search for coal.

Eliza Furnace

Straddling the Indiana/Cambria County border near the town of Vintondale, the Eliza Furnace beckons you off the trail. This intriguing pyramid-shaped stone structure is an amazing relic of southwestern Pennsylvania's industrial heritage.

Opened in 1846, this early iron furnace operated less than five years. Today, the Eliza Furnace is Pennsylvania's most well-preserved hot blast iron furnace, and it is listed on the National Register of Historic Sites. The original metal heat exchanger pipes still sit atop of the structure, which produced crude iron (also known as pig iron) for the Pittsburgh market.

Operated by a force of 90 men and boys, with 45 horses and mules, the charcoal-powered furnace produced about 1,000 tons of crude iron during its short life. The Indiana County Parks Department is currently developing an access area and some interpretive exhibits around the site.

The Eliza Furnace, located directly adjacent to the trail near Vintondale, is the best preserved hot-blast furnace in Pennsylvania.

Soon, the trail passes through a forest of trees, and thousands of wild ferns create a green floor next to the trail. At times, the atmosphere is almost tropical. The South Branch winds in and out of the woods for the next couple of miles. When you see it, you will likely notice its red hue, caused by coal mining. A group of local citizens is working to get the creeks in the area cleaned up. And, when that happens, the trail will provide excellent access for canoeing, rafting and tubing.

Near mile marker 5, you will see the town of Vintondale just ahead. Before reaching it, you will pass a massive pile of coal waste, known in this area as a "bony pile" on your left side. This particular one has been here for nearly 100 years. Beyond this point, the views open up to the surrounding hilly landscape.

Mile marker 6 signals the trail's halfway point and the trail's most outstanding feature: the Eliza furnace. You can find the White Mill Spur of the Ghost Town Trail by continuing a short distance beyond the furnace and then bearing right on a former railroad right of way. This section is developed with the exception of a 105-foot bridge, which is slated for development in spring 1995.

Just beyond the furnace, you will cross the trail's longest bridge span. This is where the North and South branches of Backlick Creek intersect, forming Backlick Creek. The bridge offers excellent views of the creek, which parallels the trail for the next few miles. You will also see many large coal piles, remnants of the area's once thriving coal industry.

At mile marker 8, you will approach another huge "bony pile," known today as the Wehrum dump. Without this pile, you might not even realize that you are passing through a ghost town. Approximately 250 houses once stood in the former coal-mining town of Wehrum. Today, barely a few foundations remain, and you will find them only if you look carefully.

When the Lackawanna Coal Company shut down its mine in the 1930s, it dismantled the entire town. In fact, workers were told that if they wanted to keep their own house, they could buy it, pack it up and move it elsewhere. Another ghost town, known as East Wheatfield, was located near mile marker 9.5. In the future, interpretive signs will explain and illustrate the area's industrial heritage.

By mile marker 10.5, the views open up to the right, revealing the rural, rolling farmland that now dominates the area. The trail

ends in Dilltown, just beyond a newly-opened bed and breakfast and gift shop.

The trailhead features a large shelter with several picnic tables, a large grill, bike racks and bathrooms—all in a pleasant green setting. Some refreshments are available at the gift shop, which is worth a stop just to see a few photos of the coal mining towns that once existed along the route of the Ghost Town Trail.

Handwritten notes:
From South
I-78
to Turn Pike
Exit # 34
go to Jim Thorpe follow Rt. 903

Lehigh Gorge State Park Trail

Handwritten notes:
turn R into Lehigh Gorge State
Park, drive over bridge & park

Endpoints: White Haven to Jim Thorpe

Location: Luzerne and Carbon Counties

Length: 25 miles

Surface: loose gravel and crushed stone

Uses: 🚶 🚲 🎣 ⛷

⛄ on certain sections

Contact: Bob Kerr or Dave Madl
RR 1, Box 81
White Haven, PA 18661
717-443-0400

◆◆◆

The Lehigh River has long been a popular family destination for whitewater rafting. Now, nearly 50,000 bicyclists, hikers and outdoor enthusiasts enjoy the river each year from one of the state's newer rail-trails. And, realizing new business opportunities, many rafting outfitters have begun shuttling bicyclists to White Haven, offering them a slight downhill grade all the way back to Jim Thorpe.

To reach the northern end of the trail without a shuttle service, take White Haven Exit 40 off Interstate 80; go to the stop sign in White Haven and turn right. Travel about a quarter-mile to the Thriftway grocery store. The trail parking lot is just beyond the store.

An active railroad crosses over the trail at the northern trailhead, which has an undeveloped parking area and an information kiosk. The trail is quite wide as it begins, and depending on the season,

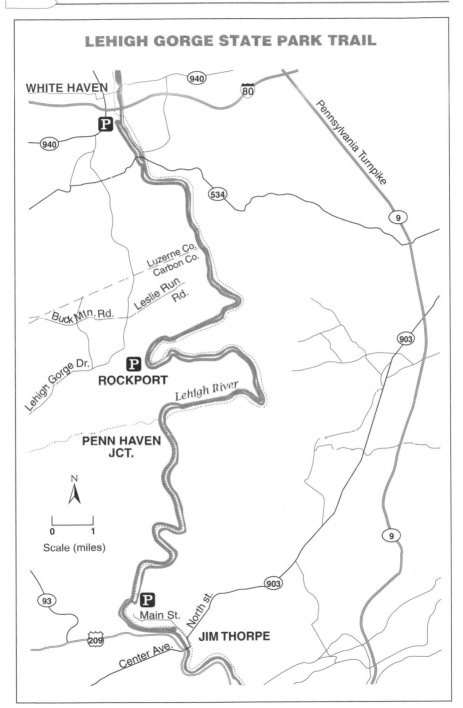

LEHIGH GORGE STATE PARK TRAIL

WHITE HAVEN

940

80

Pennsylvania Turnpike

940

534

9

Luzerne Co.
Carbon Co.

Leslie Run Rd.

Buck Mtn. Rd.

Lehigh Gorge Dr.

ROCKPORT

Lehigh River

PENN HAVEN
JCT.

N

0   1
Scale (miles)

903

9

93

209

Main St.

North St.

JIM THORPE

Center Ave.

903

you can only catch occasional glimpses of the Lehigh River below on the left side. In mid-summer the surrounding vegetation is lush and green, and by late September, the area is bursting with spectacular color. Snow can remain in the gorge through early May.

Within the first mile, you will get some brief glimpses of the river off to your left and a few hundred feet below. With any luck, you'll also spot a couple of sluggish waterfalls flowing from rocky woodlands on the right.

Near the 2.5-mile mark, you will see the remnants of a railroad bridge that once crossed the Lehigh. The trail lies on what began as a Central Railroad of New Jersey line, which serviced coal fields in the Hazelton and Wilkes-Barre area. The Lehigh Valley Railroad purchased the line in 1965 and abandoned it in 1972. The Lehigh Canal System had also dominated the area, and at one time there were 20 dams and 29 locks between White Haven and Jim Thorpe.

Over the next couple of miles, a series of small creeks—with names like Sandy Run and Hickory Run—flow into the Lehigh and are signed along the trail. At Mud Run, near mile marker 6, you can take a short winding path down to the river, where you can

Steep mountains set the stage for a great ride in the Lehigh Gorge State Park.

Active railroad tracks parallel the southern portion of the Lehigh Gorge State Park.

dip your toes on a hot day. Mud Run flows beneath a stone arch bridge under the active tracks on the opposite bank.

As you approach mile marker 7, the views in every direction get better and better. Take a moment to enjoy the dense forest all around you. By mile 8, the views open up again. The gorge you are in becomes more apparent—notice how the rocks on your right tower above you.

Prior to passing through the hamlet of Rockport, approximately nine miles south of White Haven, you will pass by one of the trail's occasional picnic tables and cross over a waterfall on a short bridge. You might also notice a set of stairs leading down to the water. This is a put-in/take out spot for whitewater rafters.

Beyond the 10-mile mark, evergreen and deciduous trees begin to envelop the trail from both sides, occasionally yielding to rocky outcroppings on the right side. You can view Stoney Creek streaming out from underneath the active tracks across the river as you approach mile 13, where the river vistas are more exposed. This generally open feeling lingers for a couple of miles, until you reach Penn Haven Junction.

A narrow gate, designed to make you dismount your bike, signals your arrival at Penn Haven Junction, where an active set of Conrail tracks suddenly parallels the trail. After passing by a short bridge, the trail bears left and crosses the active tracks.

The trail remains sandwiched between the river and the active tracks until just before the trail ends near Jim Thorpe. Generally a difference in grade separates the active tracks from the trail. Landscaping, which appears scruffy at times, reinforces the separation between the active freight tracks and the trail.

The trail surface for the next few miles seems a bit rougher than earlier parts of the trail, but the increasingly dramatic scenery will keep your mind off the extra bumps. By mile 18, it will be obvious that the trail has descended, as rocky cliffs dominate the right side. Meanwhile, the river and trail approach the same level, while the active tracks are on much higher ground.

Near mile marker 22, you will pass through the Glen Onoko Trailhead, where parking and restrooms are available. If you have time, explore this area and take a jaunt to the Glen Onoko Falls. Through the parking area, the active track temporarily veers right, and you cross over a large trestle. If you look closely, you will see an abandoned railroad tunnel, originally used by one of the four main tracks that ran through this area.

Beyond this point, the trail shares a gravel road to make the approach into Jim Thorpe. In less than a mile, you can see another abandoned steel trestle. After an additional mile—uphill—you will reach a stop sign, where you will turn right onto a paved road. Continue uphill for a short distance until you turn left at a stop light and head downhill into Jim Thorpe.

You could easily spend a day in the quaint downtown area of Jim Thorpe, a town that is coming into its own as a tourist destination. You may want to stop at the Visitors Center, housed in the center of town in an old railroad station. It offers excellent information on the railroad's role in this town. Or, you can roam around town, where you will find interesting shops, restaurants and bed-and-breakfasts.

Karen-Lee Ryan

The scenic Frankstown Branch of the Juniata River offers a pleasant backdrop to the Lower Trail.

Lower Trail

Endpoints: Williamsburg to Alfarata

Location: Blair and Huntingdon Counties

Length: 11 miles

Surface: three parallel paths, including a multi-use, hard-packed crushed limestone surface, and two original ballast and grass paths for equestrians and pedestrians

Uses: 🚶 🚲 🐎 ♿ ⛷ 🎣

Contact: Palmer Brown, President
or Jennifer Barefoot, Vice President
Rails-to-Trails of Blair County, Inc.
P.O. Box 592
Hollidaysburg, PA 16648
814-832-2400

◆◆◆

The Lower Trail is the latest reincarnation of a corridor that has had many lives. First, native Americans incorporated the route into the Kittaning Trail, which was later renamed the Frankstown Road by westward-heading pioneers. In 1832, the route was absorbed into the Pennsylvania Main Line Canal until the Petersburg Branch of the Pennsylvania Railroad took its place in the 1890s. Today, the Lower Trail is dedicated to preserving the route's rich heritage.

Originally built to support the iron industry, the railroad served the area's smelting furnaces and limestone quarries. The line operated until 1979, and a private donation later funded the trail's purchase.

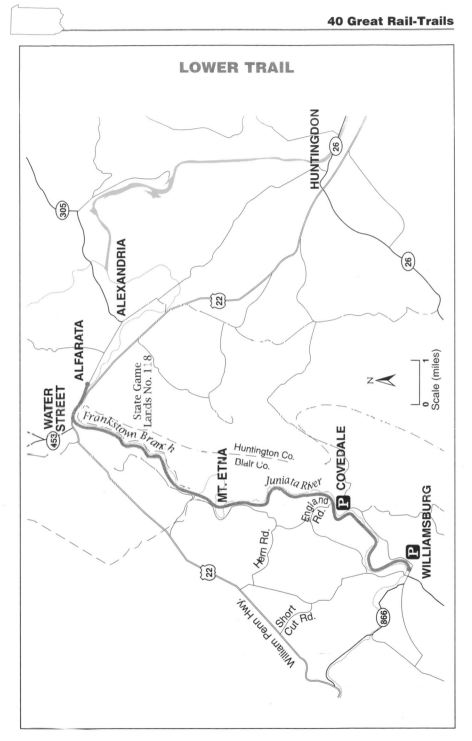

LOWER TRAIL

Rails-To-Trails of Blair County

The southern section of the Lower Trail near the Williamsburg Trailhead.

The southern trailhead of the Lower (rhymes with flower) is located at First and Liberty Streets in the tiny town of Williamsburg. To get there, take U.S Route 22 east from Altoona to State Route 866 south; follow it for three miles to Williamsburg, where 866 becomes First Street. Travel through the town's main intersection and continue two blocks to the trailhead, located on the left.

During summer and fall of 1994, the entire Lower Trail was developed with three parallel paths to support various users. A wide band of vegetation had been cleared to make way for the limestone surface, so the trail may still look a little rough around the edges as new landscaping takes hold.

With the Frankstown Branch of the Juniata River rippling on your left, the trail immediately weaves away from civilization. Steep rocks create a shallow canyon on your left, and within a mile, the river diverges from the trail. The rocks then give way to a broad view of the surrounding farmland and hilly terrain beyond.

You will cross the Frankstown Branch on the trail's first bridge at 1.5 miles. Soon you will pass an old stone house, the first of many intriguing structures and foundations that offer hints of the

corridor's past. Of course, you will need to look closely to find many of them.

By the 2.5-mile point, sheer rock faces line the left side of the trail, reminding you that the trail cuts through a steep gorge. The scenery along the next few miles of trail is quite varied: steep rocks are suddenly replaced by healthy woodlands, which at times seem to envelop the trail until more rocky outcroppings appear.

A new access point with parking has been developed at the 3.2-mile mark in the town of Covedale. And at mile 4.7, you will be passing by Lock #61, the best-preserved canal lock along the route. Just beyond the 6-mile mark, you will approach the trail's second crossing of the scenic Frankstown Branch. And, beyond the bridge, construction crews have created what can look deceivingly like a fork in the trail. Be sure to go straight (or slightly to the left) to continue on the Lower Trail.

The next couple of miles are attractive and quite peaceful. They also feature interesting remnants from the corridor's many lives. With the dramatic mountain views and the picturesque river vying for your attention, you'll need to watch carefully to see relics such as Lock #64 beyond mile 7.

Karen-Lee Ryan

The Lower Trail crosses the Frankstown Branch of the Juniata River several times.

It would be difficult to miss the remains of Goodman's Quarry at the 8.2-mile mark. Currently indicated with a wooden sign, this ghost of a structure is among the trail's many historical artifacts that will feature interpretive signs as the trail continues to develop.

Prior to mile 10, you can see additional remnants of the canal that occupied the route before the railroad replaced it. A bench made from logs is located on the left side across the trail from a sign pointing out the canal. Just beyond mile marker 10, you will see several stone foundations—including one that is nearly the length of a city block—that were part of Owen's Quarry.

The river widens as you near the northern terminus of the trail. On a hot day, you may catch a glimpse of someone in an inner tube taking advantage of the river's intermittent and refreshing rapids.

Toward the trail's northern end, you begin to parallel U.S. Route 22, located to the left. If you look to your right you will see what looks like the world's largest rock slide. This huge rock pile is actually residue from the glaciers that once covered the area. When the glaciers melted, they left this huge pile in their wake.

Within a short distance, you will cross under Route 22, and the trail continues about a half-mile to Alfarata. Eventually, trail proponents hope to continue the trail another eight miles to Huntingdon. Given the speed with which they opened the first 11 miles, they will probably have it done in no time.

This Conrail building is one of many commercial developments located along the Montour Trail.

Montour Trail

Endpoints: Coraopolis to Clairton

Location: Allegheny and Washington Counties

Length: 20 miles in three sections
(will be 55 miles when complete)

Surface: Crushed limestone

Uses:

Contact: *Coraopolis to Champion*
Tom Fix
Montour Trail Council
P.O. Box 11866
Pittsburgh, PA 15228-0866
412-831-2030

Cecil Segment
Don Berty
Montour Trail Council
P.O. Box 11866
Pittsburgh, PA 15228-0866
412-221-6406

◆ ◆ ◆

I n 1989 a group of determined citizens rallied around a new trail project. First, they created a detailed trail concept plan to mobilize community support. Next, they developed a fundraising plan, soliciting help from foundations, corporations and others. Meanwhile, another corps of volunteers cleared brush, inspected tunnels and corrected drainage problems.

The citizens' efforts paid off. The Montour Trail Council raised enough money to purchase a 55-mile rail corridor, and in less than

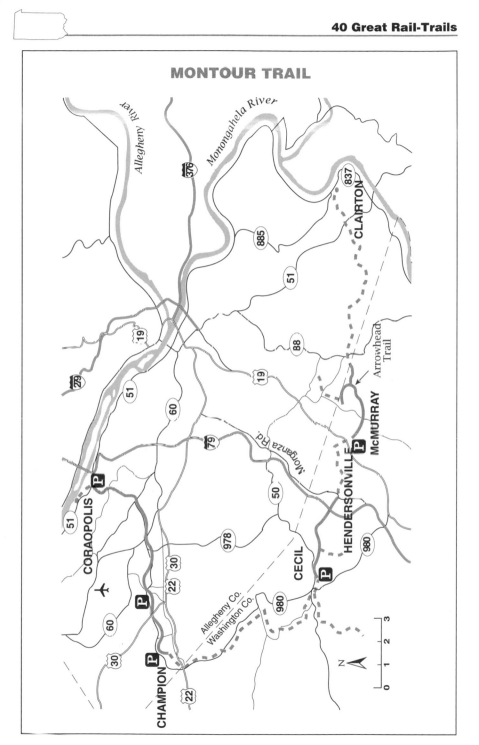

MONTOUR TRAIL

five years, these dedicated volunteers have actually built more than one-third of the Montour Trail.

Built in 1877, the Montour Railroad formed a semi-circle around the western edge of Pittsburgh. While it changed hands several times, the Montour serviced nearly 40 coal mines over the years. When the remaining coal mines shut down in the late 1970s, the Pittsburgh and Lake Erie Railroad (the Montour's final owner) began abandoning sections of track. The last segment was shut down in 1984.

Now the Montour Trail Council is giving the corridor new life. Currently, three separate portions of the Montour Trail are open to the public. One section, opened in 1985 and managed by a local township, is known as the Arrowhead Trail. It is covered separately beginning on page 23.

The other two open sections—Coraopolis to Champion and the Cecil Segment—are covered here. The remaining sections are not yet open because of rugged conditions and missing bridges. However, construction may be underway on additional sections as money permits during 1995. The Montour Trail Council can provide the latest information about trail openings and conditions.

Tom Sexton

The Montour offers interesting diversity, ranging from commercial developments to rolling countrysides.

Coraopolis to Champion

This 11.5-mile section begins just south of the Ohio River and continues through Allegheny County to the Washington County border. It is an attractive stretch of trail that combines lush vegetation, a rippling creek and a few light industrial establishments in a pleasant setting.

The northern trailhead and parking area are located less than a mile south of downtown Coraopolis off State Route 51 along the Ohio River. When traveling south on 51, take a left onto the relatively steep access road just prior to crossing under Interstate 79.

As you leave the parking lot, the trail is green and inviting, with surprisingly hilly terrain in the background. The attractive setting is soon briefly interrupted on the right as you pass by an EPA Superfund site within a half-mile. Some contaminated soil was recently removed from the fenced-off area adjacent to the trail.

At Ewings Mill, elevation 763 feet, you will cross over a bridge before approaching a firing range located adjacent to the trail. Stay alert and use common sense in this area. During hunting season, you are likely to see hunters (who are required by law to wear orange vests) in the trail's vicinity.

During the next couple of miles you will cross a shallow, meandering creek, known as Montour Run, on several small bridges. The creek, combined with sharply rising rock formations on the left, give the trail a slightly enclosed feeling, although the power lines above are a reminder that civilization remains nearby. You might also notice a few airplanes flying overhead as you travel along the trail; the Greater Pittsburgh International Airport is only a few miles away.

As you pass by mile marker 3, the surrounding area will gradually become more commercial. At an area signed Beaver Grade Road, there is a portable toilet and parking for about 10 cars.

Near 3.5, you will pass a YMCA, one of the many community resources linked together by the Montour Trail. And, judging from the large number of people using the trail at any time during the week, the trail is obviously a key transportation route connecting various community sites. The trail also skirts a number of commercial and light industrial developments, although they are occasionally hidden by short sections of steep, rocky outcroppings

Karen-Lee Ryan

The National Tunnel is a highlight of the Cecil Segment of the Montour Trail.

along the trail. The area surrounding this section of trail is undergoing rapid commercial development.

When you pass the 4-mile mark, you will be passing through Robinson Township and paralleling Montour Run Road. Soon you

will come to a wide, at-grade crossing at Park Manor Boulevard, and the commercial development continues on the other side. A Conrail office building will be visible from the trail near the State Route 60 underpass.

Near mile marker 7, you will cut through a relatively short, straight tunnel before passing by a couple of baseball diamonds. Beyond the baseball fields, which are located near the town of Imperial, some parking is available.

The newest section of trail, dedicated in October 1994, takes you into the small town of Imperial. With its long coal-mining history, this community has decided to build a small museum that will highlight the connections between the mining and railroad industries. It will be built on the site of the old depot, torn down long ago.

Once you are outside of Imperial, the trail's surroundings get progressively more rural, primarily surrounded by pasture land. Beyond the 10.5-mile mark, a reclaimed strip mine lines the trail's left side. The area has been revegetated, so it may not be apparent to the untrained eye. The trail ends less than a half-mile north of U.S. Route 22 near the tiny town of Champion.

The Montour Trail includes a side path for equestrians.

Cecil Segment

The main feature of the 4.5-mile Cecil segment of the Montour Trail is the 628-foot National Trail. This section begins in Cecil Township Park, located on State Route 50 more than a half-mile east of State Route 980 and the town of Venice. Among the park's facilities are tennis courts, picnic pavilions and restrooms. The parking lot fills quickly, so plan to use the municipal building parking lot located adjacent to the park.

To reach the trail, use the small bridge to cross over the creek that runs through Cecil Park. Bear sharply to the right at the end of the bridge and follow a short path that leads up to the Montour Trail. Once you reach the trail, you will want to bear left to head east along the trail (if you go right, you will see a "no trespassing sign" almost immediately). To get some perspective on where you are in the scheme of the 55-mile Montour Trail, use the map posted on the trail.

The elevation at this point is just over 1,000 feet, and you will continue a slow ascent as you make your way toward the National Tunnel. Within 0.3 miles, you will pass mile marker 25. Although only a few segments of the Montour Trail are open, the mile markers indicate the distance from the Montour's endpoint at Coraopolis. Along this section of trail, rolling hills are dotted with occasional residences.

By mile marker 26, the number of homes begins to decrease, and the landscape eases into a more rural tone. You might notice some equestrians along this section of trail, where a side path has been developed for their use.

Soon you will arrive at the National Tunnel, located at mile marker 27. Constructed in 1928, the tunnel was built on a curve and looks endlessly dark as you approach it. But once you have made your way inside, you will be able to see light coming from the other end.

In the winter, local residents refer to the tunnel as the National Cave because of the icy stalactites that form during cold weather. Some reach halfway to the tunnel floor! In any season, bicyclists are encouraged to walk bikes through the tunnel. Loose, chunky rocks, which help prevent pools of water from collecting in the tunnel, form the trail's surface.

Once you are on the other side of the tunnel, you will realize

the trail is now descending into Hendersonville. The trail surface is less smooth on this side of the tunnel, bearing more resemblance to gravel than to crushed limestone.

You will cross over a short bridge prior to reaching mile marker 28. Lush vegetation continues to line this relatively short section of trail, which soon crosses under Interstate 79. When you reach mile marker 29, you will see that you have nearly reached the end of this developed section. A bridge across a busy road has been removed a short distance ahead, so it is difficult to proceed much farther on this section of trail. Until more of the Montour Trail has been developed, your best bet is to turn around and retrace your steps.

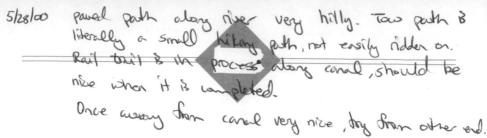

5/28/00 paved path along river very hilly. Tow path is literally a small hiking path, not easily ridden on. Rail trail is in the process along canal, should be nice when it is completed.
Once away from canal very nice, dry from other end.

National Trails Towpath Bike Trail of Palmer and Bethlehem Townships

Endpoints: Palmer to Bethlehem

Location: Northampton County

Length: 7.8 miles

Surface: Asphalt

Uses:

Contact: H. Robert Daws, Chairman
Palmer Township Board of Supervisors
P.O. Box 3039
Palmer, PA 18043
610-253-7191

◆◆◆

For more than 10 years, the short, C-shaped Towpath Bike Trail has quietly improved the lives of the 27,000 people living in Palmer and Bethlehem Townships. Virtually everyone has used the trail, which meanders through residential neighborhoods, community parks and farmland. The trail is ideally situated to access shops, schools, the public library, the regional Post Office and other community resources. And, people from throughout eastern Pennsylvania have discovered this pleasant rail-trail and its link to the 32-mile Lehigh Canal National Recreation Trail.

The Towpath Bike Trail incorporates the history of two railroads. The Central Railroad of New Jersey built its Allentown to Easton track in the late 1850s to transport anthracite coal. The

NATIONAL TRAILS TOWPATH BIKE TRAIL OF PALMER AND BETHLEHEM TOWNSHIPSHIPS

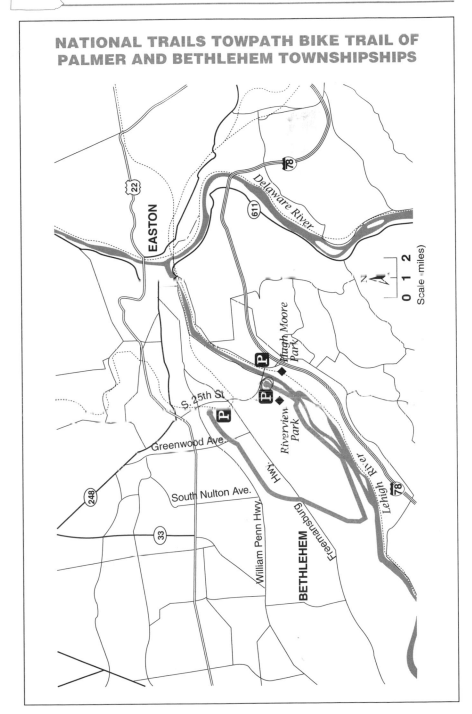

Bethlehem and Easton Interurban built its trolley line soon there-after. Reading Railroad took over both companies in 1901, although Conrail was the abandoning railroad in 1976.

Funding for trail acquisition and construction came from a one-time federal rails-to-trails grant program. The townships purchased the land in 1979 and dedicated the trail in 1981.

The trail's southern tip cuts through Riverview Park, adjacent to the Lehigh River. To get to this part of the trail, take U.S. Route 22 east from State Route 33 to 25th Street South. Travel approxi-mately 2 miles on 25th Street and turn right on Lehigh Street; make a right into the Palmer Riverview Park parking lot.

The first section of trail travels through this large community park. It offers a sizable, wheelchair-accessible fishing pier, numer-ous picnic tables, grills, tennis courts, lighted baseball diamonds and the area's first and only boccie ball court. Another park is also nearby: about a half-mile from Riverview Park off 25th street on the opposite side of the Lehigh River, the Hugh Moore Park offers access to the Lehigh Canal Trail. The park also offers several other trails, seasonal canal boat rides and picnic areas.

The National Trails Towpath Bike Trail winds between Riverview Park and the Lehigh River for a short stretch. As you make your

The trail begins in Palmer's family-oriented Riverview Park.

way to the edge of the park, you will descend a hill. It puts you virtually at the same level as the wide Lehigh River, which is dammed just a short distance up the trail. You will pass Chain Dam, which offers good views of the river, within a half-mile of the parking lot. Next, you will cross under an old stone arch overpass, quickly followed by a steep, uphill climb.

When you get to the top, the trail occupies one lane of Chain Dam Road. The other lane is one-way for car traffic. As you travel along this road, generally downhill, you cut through an established single-family-home residential area. Dense trees line the left edge of the trail, blocking most views to the Lehigh River.

Approximately 2.5 miles from Riverview Park, the trail bears left and becomes its own corridor again. This portion of the trail is wooded and pleasant. You catch sporadic glimpses of the surrounding farmland, and you will probably notice an inactive industrial area on either side of the trail before it crosses over U.S. Route 22. From this refurbished railroad trestle, you can enjoy some panoramic views of the area.

Next you will cross Sheridan Road, quickly followed by Stone's Crossing Road, where several shops and restaurants are located. The trail then passes behind a residential area and through Prospect Park. Here, you will find a portable toilet, a playground and picnic tables. Fairview Park, a larger community park with extensive parking, is located just a short distance up the trail. Soon you cross Minc Lane Road, where some new housing developments are springing up.

The Towpath Bike Trail continues linking resources together when it cuts directly behind Palmer's busy Post Office, located at Greenwood Avenue. A large shopping plaza is also nearby. Next, you will pass some new residences, followed by an area of light industry area before the trail ends at William Penn Highway across the street from Easton Area High School.

Oil Creek State Park Trail

Endpoints: Petroleum Centre to Drake Oil Well Museum
near Titusville

Location: Crawford and Venango Counties

Length: 9.7 miles

Surface: Asphalt

Uses: 🚶 🚲 🛼 ♿ 🎣 ⛷️

Contact: Douglas Finger, Park Manager
Oil Creek State Park
RR1, Box 207
Oil City, PA 16301
814-676-5915

◆◆◆

As you travel through the serene Oil Creek State Park, it is hard to imagine that you are traveling through "the valley that changed the world." In 1859, Colonel Edwin L. Drake struck oil near Titusville and created the world's first oil well. Within two years, hundreds of oil wells were erected in the area, producing thousands of barrels every day. By the mid-1870s the oil boom in northwestern Pennsylvania ended, but the discovery changed the world forever.

The Oil Creek Railroad had only one purpose when it opened in 1863: to transport the oil being drilled throughout the area. But, the boom was short-lived and the railroad's purpose soon subsided. Today, it has new life as a bicycle trail through Oil Creek State Park, which is dedicated to telling the story of the early petroleum industry.

To reach the park, take Pennsylvania 8 approximately three miles north of Oil City and through Rouseville to State Route 1007,

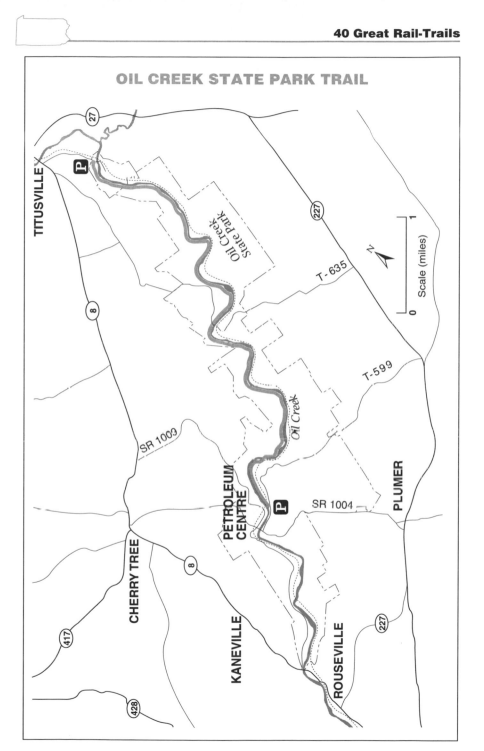

OIL CREEK STATE PARK TRAIL

which begins at the park's boundary. Travel just over two miles and take a sharp right turn over Oil Creek to reach a large parking area near the park office and visitor center.

This area is known as Petroleum Centre, and it once boasted a population of 5,000 people. In the 1860s you would have found a whiskey mill, an oil refinery, hotels, stores, saloons and theaters. Today, picnic tables, shade shelters and bathrooms are the highlights.

Following signs to the park's bicycle trail, you will initially parallel Oil Creek on a paved road for the first half-mile until the trail veers left along the creek. You will cross an active set of railroad tracks. Between May and October, the Oil Creek and Titusville Railroad operates a 26-mile tourist train on many weekends. Throughout the park, you can also take advantage of more than 30 miles of hiking trails and 15 miles of cross-country skiing trails.

The trail is pleasant from the start, with the calmly flowing creek on your left and the woods on your right. Picnic tables occasionally dot the trail as do interesting historical markers that explain the area's history. It's worth taking the time to read the signs, which often feature pictures and drawings of what the area looked like in its industrial heyday.

Tom Sexton

Scenic view of the Oil Creek River near Titusville.

Beyond mile marker 1.5, you will make your only crossing over Oil Creek. Once on the other side, you get a clearer sense of the gorge through which you are traveling.

The next couple of miles feature surprisingly dense woods given that oil enthusiasts had virtually cleared the area's vegetation in their zeal to find black gold. Several historical markers provide additional details about the individuals who came to the area and photographs reveal the toll their efforts took on the land. Today, the vegetation is recovering, and hemlocks are abundant throughout the gorge.

By mile marker 3, Oil Creek briefly comes back into sight, and benches are thoughtfully placed for your viewing enjoyment. Some of the best vistas are near mile 3.5, as the creek takes a wide bend. In this area, you might also see (or more likely hear) a wild turkey or some of the many songbirds that are common along the route.

A large picnic shelter, picnic tables, bike racks and bathrooms are located just before mile marker 5. One of the trail's few road crossings is located at mile 5, where parking is available. Just a short distance up the trail, a historical marker describes an oil pipeline that was constructed through the area.

By mile 6, which features an overlook with some benches, the creek again comes into view on the right. At the same time, rocky banks appear on the left, highlighting the steepness of Oil Creek Gorge. The steepness soon catches up with the trail, which has an increasingly noticeable grade beginning about 6.5 miles from Petroleum Centre on the way to Titusville.

Remnant foundations from the former town of Boughton, which once housed a lumber mill and later an "acidworks," are located near mile marker 7.5. A historical marker provides the interesting details. By this time, the creek has skirted away from the trail again and makes only intermittent appearances between here and the trail's end beyond mile marker 9.

As you complete the last leg of the trail, you will come down into a large parking lot with picnic tables. If you have any time to spare, continue through the parking lot, cross the bridge to the right, and continue to the Drake Oil Well Museum. This historic site commemorates the world's first oil discovery. The museum offers many oil-related exhibits, and the surrounding grounds feature several buildings that tell the story of the discovery and drilling of oil.

great trail! 8/01

Plainfield Township Trail

Endpoints: Stockertown to Pen Argyl

Location: Northampton County

Length: 6.7 miles

Surface: Crushed stone and gravel

Uses:

Contact: Jenny Koehler, Treasurer
Plainfield Board of Supervisors
517 Getz Road
Nazareth, PA 18064
610-759-6944

◆◆◆

I n the future, the Plainfield Township Trail could connect with seven other trails—including the Appalachian Trail—to create a continuous trail network from the Lehigh and Delaware Valleys to the Pocono Mountains. Located between Allentown and the Poconos, the Plainfield Township Trail currently offers quiet isolation in a rural setting. And, the scenic Bushkill Creek, with its soothing rippling action, parallels the trail's entire length.

Built by the Bangor and Portland Railway, this corridor opened in 1880 to transport slate from nearby quarries. In 1909, the rail line merged with the Delaware, Lackawanna and Western Railroad. The last steam locomotive traversed the route in 1953. The line, which Conrail purchased in 1976, remained active until its abandonment in 1981. Plainfield Township purchased the line in 1987 and converted it into a trail.

The get to the southern trailhead, take State Route 33 north five miles from U.S. 22 and then take 191 north toward Stockertown.

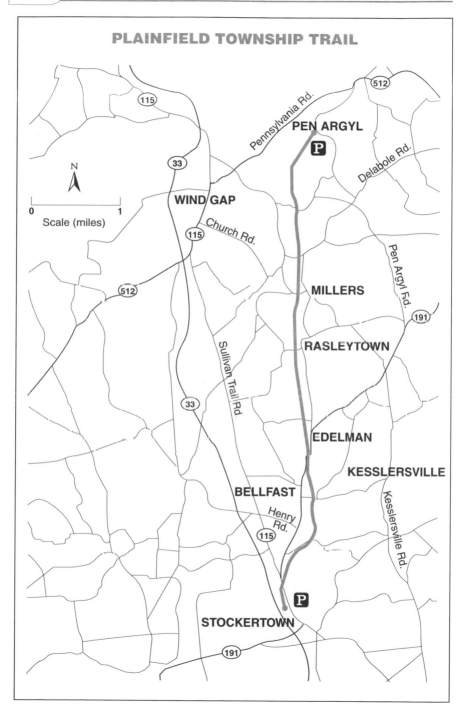

PLAINFIELD TOWNSHIP TRAIL

Tom Sexton

The Plainfield Township Trail offers a serene, pastoral setting.

Travel 0.7 miles on 191 to the trailhead, located on the right. The parking lot is adjacent to a small power sub-station. Do not use the parking lot's sparse appearance to gauge the trail. Almost as soon as you set out on the trail, you will see—or at least hear—the Bushkill Creek, more than 50 feet below on the right. Within a half-mile, you will get your first rural vistas, as farmhouses come into view on the right.

Trees line most of the trail's left side. And the Bushkill darts in and out of view on the right until it settles into a parallel path alongside the trail within 1.5 miles. The trail surface, which starts as hard-packed red stones, soon gives way to a rougher ballast surface.

As you near the two-mile mark, you will see remnants of the slate industry that once prospered in this area. After passing a few residences, you will cross Route 191 at grade—use caution. Soon you will pass by an intriguing stone structure that once served as a schoolhouse.

For the next couple of miles, the trail heads virtually due north, and you will cross the meandering Bushkill Creek and its tributaries several times. The red stone surface resumes near 2.5 miles, where

you begin to see views of the Pocono foothills in the foreground. Oaks, maples and poplars define the trail's border in a peacefully remote setting.

Just before 3.5 miles, several picnic tables have been tucked into the woods on both sides of the trail. The creek continues to creep in and out of view, and just beyond the four-mile mark, a double bridge span crosses the Bushkill. Views from the bridge are excellent, and so is the fishing. Soon, you will cross Knitters Hill Road, where another trail access area and parking lot are located. The gates erected here and at other road crossings to keep out motorized vehicles are poorly designed, making passage with a bike cumbersome.

The landscape adjacent to the trail is now rolling farmland with occasional single-family homes. By mile five, you begin a modest ascent toward Pen Argyl—an incline that gets more noticeable when the surface changes to a thicker gravel. Within a mile, you will pass a handful of slate piles—one looks like a small mountain. These are remnants of the area's quarries, one of which is still in operation.

Before the trail's northern endpoint, signs will indicate a truck crossing. Trucks cross the trail here as they transport slate from one side of the quarry to the other. Consequently, the surface is extremely muddy and rutted at times. The trail's northern parking lot is just beyond the truck crossing, prior to another slate mountain that appears to sit on the corridor just ahead.

From this point, you are a short distance from the small town of Pen Argyl, where you will find a few shops and restaurants. To get there, take a left onto Pen Argyl Road to West Main Road.

Samuel Justus Recreational Trail

Endpoints: Franklin to Oil City

Location: Venango County

Length: 5.8 miles

Surface: Asphalt

Uses: 🚶 🚴 🐎 ♿ 🛼 🎣 ⛷

Contact: Richard A. Castonguay
Secretary
Cranberry Township
P.O. Box 378
Seneca, PA 16346
814-676-8812

◆◆◆

Named after the foundation in Oil City that paid for the trail's development, the Samuel Justus Trail was the first section of rail-trail developed along Pennsylvania's Allegheny River. And, fortunately for trail lovers, it seems to have sparked rapid rail-trail development along the river's edge. In 1994, the first five miles of the 15-mile Allegheny River Trail were developed. It connects with the Justus Trail at the Franklin trailhead and extends south toward Brandon (see page 21). And, a 55-mile rail-trail project is also underway along the river in Armstrong County.

Originally the Allegheny Valley Railroad, this corridor was developed in 1868 to connect the burgeoning oil industry in Oil City to Pittsburgh. But, the oil wells dried up by the mid 1870s, and the line continued to operate independently until the Pennsylvania Railroad system absorbed it in 1910. Conrail later took over the line, and abandoned it in 1984.

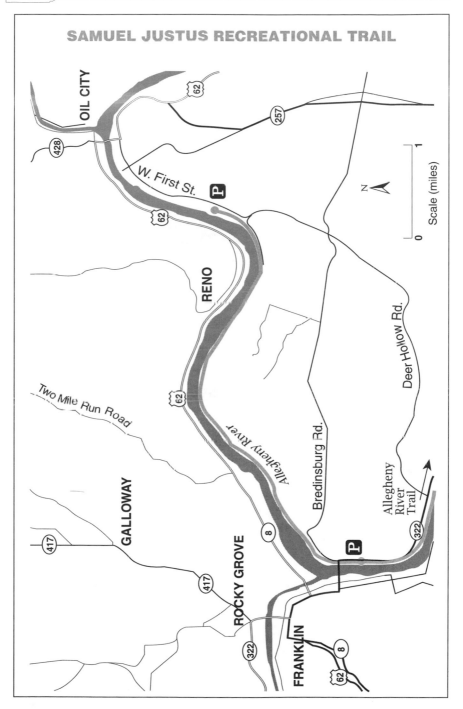

SAMUEL JUSTUS RECREATIONAL TRAIL

This trail and the surrounding area are included in one of Pennsylvania's Industrial Heritage Corridors because of the role this area had in the state's short-lived oil boom. While traveling along this former railroad route, you will see many remnants of the oil industry, including long-abandoned oil pumps.

The Justus Trail and the Allegheny River Trail share a common trailhead, located in a large parking lot alongside U.S Route 322 just east of Franklin. In the lot, you will find picnic tables, benches, portable toilets and great views of the Allegheny River. As soon as you begin the Justus Trail, you will cross under Route 322 and pass by a bicycle rental shop that also stocks snacks and beverages.

Power lines parallel the trail for the first mile, after which they turn away from the trail. Beyond this point, the trail takes on a more pastoral tone, pleasantly isolated in a small gorge. As you travel toward the once-bustling Oil City, the wide Allegheny River flows along on your left side, and steep, rocky bluffs line your right side.

Distance markers are numerous along this trail, with a marker for every half-mile and every kilometer. You will even see a few of the original stone railroad mile markers. Prior to mile marker 3,

A few original mile markers still remain on the Samuel Justus Trail.

you will see a post marked "126," which once indicated to railroad crews that they were 126 miles from Pittsburgh.

By mile marker 3, the woods have begun to separate you from the river, and the steep rocks on the right have disappeared. The river views begin to open up again beyond mile marker 4. And you are now in an area that has relics from the oil boom days, including several oil pumps.

Picnic tables dot the trail until mile marker 4.5, where a large picnic area is nestled between the river and the trail. This large green area offers many shade trees, abundant picnic tables and a few grills. If you didn't pack a lunch, stop here anyway and just enjoy the view.

The trail continues for a little more than a mile, ending at a trail parking lot adjacent to a water treatment plant. To get to Oil City, turn right at the end of the parking lot, go less than two blocks to West First Street, and turn left. Within two miles, you will be in downtown Oil City.

Once a busy commercial center, Oil City is now a sleepy town with a few banks, restaurants and shops. The many large Victorian homes that still line the streets, make the trip into town worthwhile.

Determined trail advocates are looking at routes that will someday link the Samuel Justus Trail with the Oil Creek State Park Trail (see page 57). Given the success of trail development along the Allegheny River, these advocates seem destined to succeed.

Schuylkill River Trail

Endpoints: Valley Forge to Philadelphia

Location: Montgomery and Philadelphia Counties

Length: 11.5 miles of a 21-mile trail are on an abandoned rail line

Surface: Asphalt and original ballast

Uses: 🚶 🚴 ♿ 🛼 ⛷ 🎣

🚴 on certain sections

Contact: John H. Wood
Chief of Open Space Planning
Montgomery County Planning Commission
Courthouse
Norristown, PA 19404
610-278-3736

◆◆◆

Extending from the Valley Forge National Historical Park to the historic City of Philadelphia, this trail is a popular destination for residents of and visitors to the City of Brotherly Love. Every year nearly a quarter-million people enjoy this greenway along the scenic Schuylkill River.

Abandoned by Conrail in the late 1970s, this corridor was sold to the Philadelphia Electric Company. Montgomery County negotiated an easement with the utility company, and in 1979 began building the trail in phases. Originally operated by the Pennsylvania Railroad, the line serviced the area's limestone quarries and coal mines, which fueled the iron and steel industries.

Before you get on the trail, you may want to spend some time at Valley Forge National Historical Park, which highlights the six-

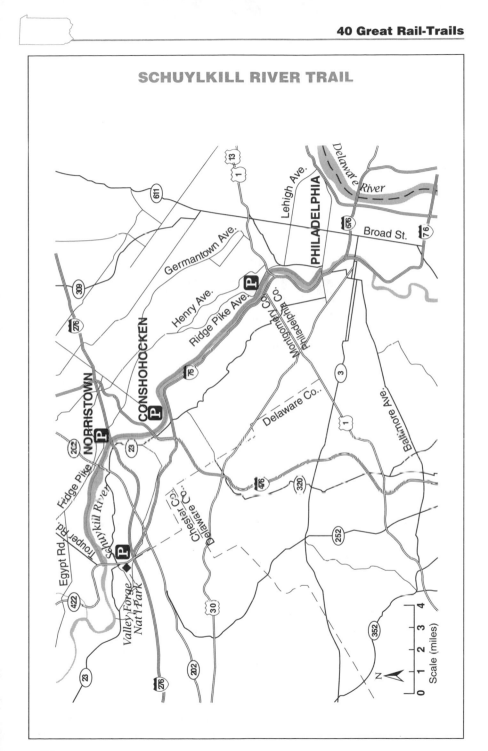

SCHUYLKILL RIVER TRAIL

Karen-Lee Ryan

The Schuylkill River Trail, a few miles west of Center City
Philadelphia, is popular with a variety of users.

month encampment of General George Washington's Army during
the winter of 1777 and 1778. A self-guided tour begins at the
Visitors' Center, where you can get information on other attractions
and trails within the park.

To get to Valley Forge, take Interstate 76 (Schuylkill Express-
way) west from Interstate 476. Take U.S. Route 202 south for 200
yards to U.S. Route 422. Proceed four miles, exit onto State Route
23 and into the National Historical Park. The parking area has
restrooms, phones and picnic tables.

To reach the Schuylkill River Trail, follow the paved trail from
the parking lot around the Visitors' Center and get onto the multi-
use trail for almost a half-mile. Following posted signs, you will
cross State Route 23. Then you will cross over the river using a
very narrow bike lane on the Route 422 Bridge. When you get to
the end of that bridge, you will bear right to begin the trail. If you
look left, you will see that the corridor continues but is not paved.
The trail is slated for an extension five miles west from this point,
with a projected completion date of fall 1995.

The trail is an instant delight with its canopy of trees and quiet setting. The first attraction you may want to explore along the way is Riverfront Park in Norristown, about three miles east on the trail. Accessible from Haws Avenue, the park offers a scenic loop trail, picnic tables and excellent views of the river.

After passing several industrial buildings near mile marker 4, the trail cuts directly through the Norristown Transportation Center—home to a light rail station and numerous busses. The Schuylkill River Trail's connection to the Transportation Center means local residents have the opportunity to bike or walk to public transportation. About halfway through Norristown, the county seat of Montgomery County, a 1.3-mile, on-road detour bypasses an active stretch of railroad track.

Signs will lead you left from the trail onto Ford Street for one block, where you will turn right onto East Main Street. After more than a half-mile on Main, turn right onto Conshohocken Road and go another half-mile. Then go under two overpasses and bear right into what looks like an industrial park. You will pick up the trail again on the left. The county recently reached a final agreement with Conrail to move the trail next to the active railroad tracks,

In-line skating competes with bicycling as the common activity on the Schuylkill River Trail.

Karen-Lee Ryan

The Schuylkill River unites many forms of transportation.

making the detour unnecessary. This rerouting could take place as early as the summer of 1995.

For a short distance you will be passing through an industrial area. But by mile marker 6, a rocky gorge quickly envelops the trail's left side, creating a sense of pleasant isolation. More industrial development comes into view within a mile as you approach Conshohocken, which was a booming steel town in the early 1900s.

The trail again goes off-grade for about 1.5 miles in Conshohocken, although the agreement with Conrail should eliminate this detour by mid-1995. Signs will lead you left from the trail uphill for two blocks, where you will turn right onto First Avenue. If you are hungry or need a break, this area offers plenty of places to stop. After crossing Harry Street, you will bear left onto Springmill Avenue. Stay on it for nearly a mile until you reach Lime Street, where you will turn right. After a block, turn left onto Hector Street and then right onto Station Avenue, which leads you to a parking lot. Take a left onto the trail just before the active tracks and continue your journey to Philadelphia.

The next mile is a very pleasant section of trail, with rocky formations appearing on your left side and good river views off to

the right. In a little more than a mile, the paved trail comes to an end. To get to the Manayunk Canal Towpath, bear right and cut over to a parallel road—Nixon Street. Pass Shawmont Avenue and an old railroad station, and then cross a set of railroad tracks. Soon you will be on the cobblestones that lead to the towpath.

Mountain bikes are recommended on this narrow, gravel-surfaced section of the Schuylkill River Greenway. The first point of interest along the way is Flat Rock Dam. Within two miles, you will cross a series of boardwalks along the trail, signaling your arrival into the recently refurbished town of Manayunk. Main Street, replete with shops and restaurants, is less than two blocks from the trail. Or, if you go a bit further to the end of the towpath, you will find yourself at the sizable Farmer's Market. In addition to fresh produce booths, many restaurants have set up small stands to sell their culinary delights. Restrooms are also available.

If you plan to continue into Philadelphia, you will need to travel on streets for a couple of miles until you reach the Fairmount Park trail system that leads you directly into downtown. To get to Philadelphia, take Main Street out of Manayunk until you see signs for Kelly Road. Take a sharp right up the ramp to Kelly Road and follow it for a short time until you see the paved Fairmount Trail on the right. The trail runs between Kelly Drive and the Schuylkill River.

This part of the trail, paved with asphalt, may be the most heavily-used section of the Schuylkill River Trail. On summer days, the trail is teeming with in-line skaters, bicyclists and runners, and the green spaces between the river and the trail are jam-packed with people of all ages. Take some time to enjoy the views.

If you continue on the trail for several miles, you will eventually reach the Art Museum. From there, you can continue on-street (following signs) to many of Philadelphia's historic attractions, including Independence Hall.

Stony Valley Railroad Grade

Endpoints: Dauphin to Lebanon Reservoir

Location: Dauphin, Lebanon and Schuylkill Counties

Length: 17.4 miles

Surface: Crushed stone

Uses: 🚶 🚴 🐎 ♿ 🎣 ⛷ 🛷

Contact: Chief
Federal-State Coordination Division
Pennsylvania Game Commission
2001 Elmerton Avenue
Harrisburg, Pennsylvania 17110-9797
(717) 787-9612

◆◆◆

As you travel the Stony Valley Railroad Grade, it's hard to imagine that this lush green forest of oak, white pine, hemlock, beech and maple didn't exist when the last of the miners and lumbermen left the area decades ago. Located in 41,500 acres of state game land, the Stony Valley trail is surrounded by wilderness that has rebounded remarkably. In addition to the multi-use trail, the area provides habitat for many animals and preserves what remains of the former mining towns.

Named St. Anthony's Wilderness by Moravian missionaries who came to the region in 1742 to convert native tribes, the Stony Creek area grew rapidly. Five bustling towns totaling 3,000 people sprouted up after the discovery of coal in 1824: Rausch Gap, Yellow Spring Gap, Gold Mine, Rattling Run, and Cold Springs. The Schuylkill and Susquehanna Railroad soon followed.

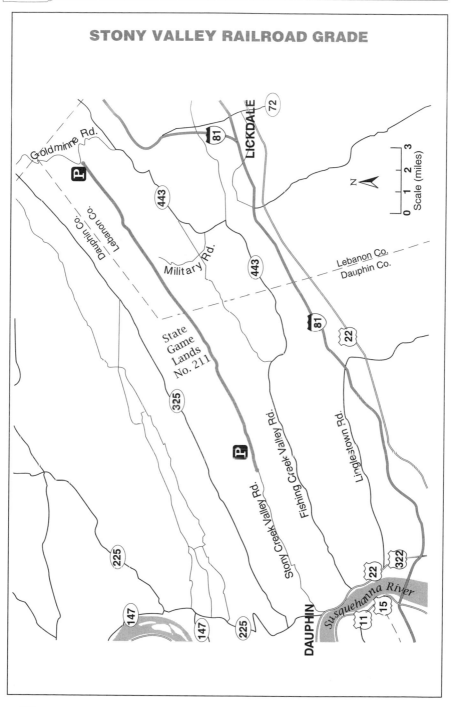

STONY VALLEY RAILROAD GRADE

Constructed between 1850 and 1854 the railroad transported coal to the river canals and tourists to Cold Springs' famous mineral water. In its heyday, the mineral spring water was so popular that a 200-room resort hotel was built to accommodate the wealthy Philadelphians who came for the healing waters. When the mines were abandoned, the lumber industry took over. By 1944, the land was stripped, the railroad abandoned and the hotel burned as the last residents departed.

Years later, the railroad was converted to a trail by the Pennsylvania Game Commission, and in 1980 Stony Creek became the first area protected under Pennsylvania's Wild and Scenic Rivers Program. As you travel along the trail today, you may hear the gurgling of an underground stream that flows over rocks in the Rattling Run area or the ghostly moans of a headless railroad worker said to stalk the trail at night.

To reach the trail's eastern terminus, take Interstate 81 to Exit 30 (Lickdale). Take State Route 72 north to State Route 443 to Gold Mine Road, which veers off 443 to the left. Follow Gold Mine Road to the State Game Lands entrance on the left.

As you head west from the Gold Mine Road entrance, the old railbed rises nearly six feet above the forest floor. The forest is primarily hemlock in this area. A few side paths, posted with "No snowmobiling" signs, lead off into the forest. At 1.2 miles, the first of many keystone-shaped concrete markers appears to your right. You will see these old remnants, which served as markers for the railroad, at numerous points along the trail. In winter, you get open vistas to the north, exposing an adjacent ridge. This is a good visual reminder of the ridge and valley systems through which you are traveling.

After 1.5 miles, you cross Sand Spring, a small creek that pools to form a trailside pond. For nearly two miles, the trail is arrow straight as it proceeds slightly uphill. As the trail rises, you can look down on small ponds and less defined wetlands.

Before you reach the 3.5-mile mark, the trail finally makes a sweeping turn to the north and then resumes its straight path. Soon, you will arrive at the abandoned town of Rausch Gap, where you will notice a lime release station near the creek. Past mining operations have increased the acidity of the creek, and the limestone helps bring the water back into balance. Here you can

You will pass over this attractive stone arch at Rausch Gap.

also visit the town's cemetery, where headstones date back to 1854, by following a trail to the south. Also in this area, the Stony Valley Railroad Grade crosses the Appalachian Trail.

As you reach mile four, you will have descended somewhat, but you are about to resume an uphill grade. Soon the trail will be nearly 30 feet above the forest floor. Through the trees, you can see a short railroad siding to the north. This extra track next to the original rail line permitted railcars to pass as others moved up the hill.

In this area, you may see—and will certainly hear—a few jets from the Fort Indiantown Gap Air Field. Army pilots practice their landings and take-offs on a regular basis, at times flying directly overhead.

Beyond mile 5.5, the trail flattens out again and the Cold Springs Trail, a rugged hiking trail, crosses the railbed. Unfortunately, the remarkably well-preserved Cold Springs Railroad Station was removed and sent to a landfill in 1994, much to the displeasure of historians and trail users. However, you can still see the remains of an old hotel.

For the next few miles the trail is straight, with a slight downhill grade. At mile eight, you come upon two small wooden plank bridges near the abandoned village of Yellow Springs. Named for the yellowish mine discharge running from atop the mountain, Yellow Springs still has the foundations of several structures. You may see deer, turkey and grouse in the area.

By the ninth mile of the trail, you've entered Dauphin County and the forest becomes predominantly white pine. There's another climb and a boulder field. Then the trail flattens out and resumes its direct path, only to give way to yet another climb. By mile 10, you become aware of the adjacent Stony Creek for which the railroad and the trail were named. It's barely visible through the evergreens, but the rush of its water is audible.

This area of the trail tends to get muddy and rutted and can be quite rough if you are on a bike with anything narrower than a hybrid tire. The washboard effect—ruts left when the railroad ties were removed—will remind you of the trail's previous use as you bump along. The surface ranges from finely crushed rock to inch-thick chunks.

Nearly 10.5 miles into the trip, the railbed makes another turn to the north, with the trail now again above the forest floor.

You'll see a lovely wetland area to the left with wood duck boxes and signs of beavers' work on trees. The trail soon becomes even and uniform, with grass on both sides. By mile 11, Stony Creek becomes your constant companion, and the forest is a mix of hemlock, beech and rhododendron. Just beyond mile 11, there's a great spot for soaking your feet on a warm summer day.

Soon the creek turns away, but the underground stream known as Rattling Run appears. The old stagecoach road that ran from Dauphin to Pottsville is located just north of Rattling Run. When you see Stagecoach Road, it will be hard to imagine that any stagecoach could have made the climb. If you choose to attempt the rigorous ride or hike up Stagecoach Road (marked by a sign "To the Monument"), you will find the Stony Mountain Fire Tower at the top of the ridge in 2.5 miles. The vistas are beautiful and the sidetrip worthwhile, but use extreme caution on the way down.

Back on the trail, hemlocks on either side create a dark, tunnel-like environment. Before mile 14, the trail curves north and continues slightly uphill. Soon Stony Creek returns to your side, providing another opportunity to dip your toes.

Beyond mile 15, you will pass the Water Tank Trail that leads to the top of the ridge. Just beyond it, a small grove of spruce trees invite you to take a break underneath them. Just before 17.5 miles, you come to another gate, signaling the end of the Stony Valley Railroad Grade. A State Game Lands parking area is located here. However, you can continue on this quiet dirt road for nearly five miles until you reach the paved section of Stony Valley Road.

Switchback Trail

Endpoints: Jim Thorpe to Summit Hill

Location: Carbon County

Length: 18 miles

Surface: Original ballast, ranging from a dirt-gravel mix to large chunks of rock

Uses:

Contact: Dennis J. DeMara
Park Director
Carbon County Park and Recreation
Department
625 Lentz Trail Road
Jim Thorpe, PA 18229
717-325-3669

◆◆◆

The Switchback Trail may have the most interesting history of any rail-trail. Powered only by gravity, the Switchback Railroad was the nation's second operating railroad when it opened in 1827. When the rail route became unnecessary, the line was converted into "the world's first roller coaster." Today, the Switchback Trail is a semi-loop trail, with some steep grades cutting through rugged terrain. This is not your average rail-trail!

Built by pioneers Josiah White and Erskine Hazard, the Switchback Railroad opened in 1827 for one purpose: to haul coal from the mine in Summit Hill to the Lehigh Canal in the town of Mauch Chunk (now the town of Jim Thorpe). Mules pulled empty railroad cars from the Lehigh Canal uphill to the mine. Once the cars were full of coal, gravity carried them all the way back to the canal.

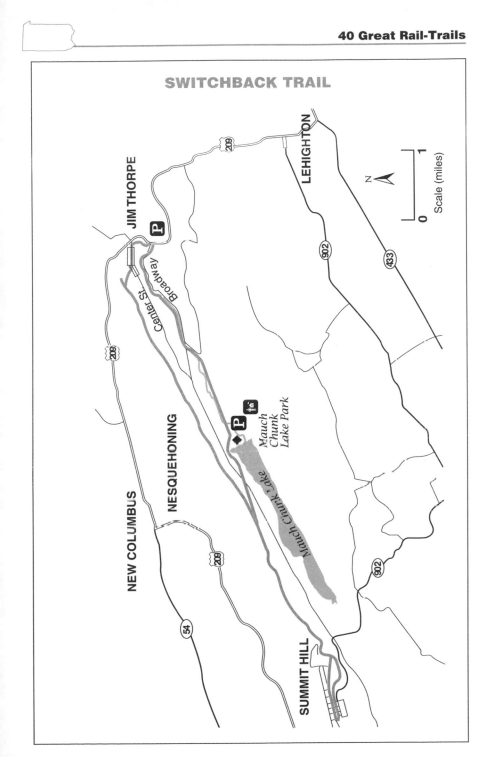

SWITCHBACK TRAIL

Karen-Lee Ryan

The Switchback Railroad Trail offers excellent views of the attractive Mauch Chunk Lake.

By the early 1870s, major railroads rendered the Switchback obsolete, so it was turned into a tourist attraction and dubbed "the world's first roller coaster." Attracting people from around the world, it became America's second most popular tourist attraction after Niagara Falls. The Depression put the Switchback out of business in 1933.

While several attempts have been made to rejuvenate the passenger train over the years, the Carbon County Park Department manages the corridor as a multi-use trail. In the early 1980s, the rugged Switchback Trail was declared a National Recreation Trail. Today it is especially popular with mountain bicyclists.

Many people begin their Switchback journey from the Jersey Central Railroad Station in downtown Jim Thorpe, located eight miles north of the Pennsylvania Turnpike (Route 9) on U.S. Route 209. Ample parking is available at this railroad station turned visitors' center. To get to the trail, travel a couple of blocks west on Broadway, and turn right at the Opera House onto the appropriately named Hill Road. In less than a half-mile uphill, you will turn left onto the trail.

The first mile of trail is fairly rough, with a few tree roots and

muddy sections mixed with occasional chunks of rock. This area is surprisingly wooded, considering that the surrounding area was extensively logged during the first half of the 1800s. Within a mile, you will cross over a concrete bridge with an orange gate before coming to Lentz Trail Highway (State Route 3012). Turn right, and within 0.1 miles the trail continues on the opposite side of the road and heads back into the woods.

With a smoother surface, this section of the Switchback is significantly wider and more pleasant. The Mauch Chunk Creek ripples off to your right, and you are surrounded by a young forest of predominantly oak, hickory and birch. Within a mile, you will cross a wooden bridge. Nearby, a picnic table offers a wonderful lunch spot.

Soon the trail bears sharply right and seems to disappear in the grassy expanse that opens up views of the surprisingly large and delightful Mauch Chunk Lake. You are now on the outskirts of Mauch Chunk Lake Park, about four miles from downtown Jim Thorpe. Continue past the park manager's residence to the park's paved entrance.

In the 2,300-acre park—home to the three-mile long Mauch Chunk Lake—you can swim, fish, camp, picnic or (during winter months) rent cross-country skis. The park also offers a small convenience store near the boat launch and a refreshment stand near the beach area. Restrooms are also available. The park headquarters, where you will find park information and friendly people, is located in the log cabin near the park's main entrance.

To continue on the Switchback Trail, cross Lentz Trail Highway and bear left on the trail. This section of trail remains pleasantly wooded, with a slight uphill grade. Within a mile, you will see attractive stonework on either side of the trail. This handiwork is the remains of an old stone trestle that once crossed overhead. This is an important feature to watch for because it signals the crossroads of the Switchback Trail.

Just beyond these trestle remains, you can continue straight and gradually uphill for another 3.5 miles to Summit Hill. Or, you can take a very sharp right turn and begin the four-mile moderate ascent to Mount Pisgah. (This segment should only be attempted by experienced mountain bicyclists or hikers. The top of the mountain puts you about 1.5 very steep miles from your starting point to

If you travel up Mount Pisgah, you will need to negotiate this rocky ledge.

complete the Switchback loop.) Or, if you are in good shape and want the longest ride—a total of 18 miles start to finish—you can head to Summit Hill, double back to this old stone trestle, ride up to Mount Pisgah and complete the 1.5 miles downhill.

Jim Thorpe, Pennsylvania

First named Coalville in 1815, this settlement along the Lehigh River was later renamed Mauch Chunk, only to change its name again in the mid-1950s to Jim Thorpe. An interesting town with unique names and an intriguing history, Jim Thorpe is a place worth visiting.

A native American name for "Bear Mountain," Mauch Chunk played a key role in eastern Pennsylvania's anthracite coal industry throughout the 1800s. English, Welsh and Irish immigrants developed the town, which was selected as the county seat for the newly-created Carbon County in 1843. For the next 50 years Mauch Chunk flourished, fueled by the coal, lumber and railroad industries. Elaborate Victorian homes, churches and community buildings soon filled the surrounding hillsides of Mauch Chunk, Upper Mauch Chunk and East Mauch Chunk.

By the 1920s, with the coal and timber depleted, the region's economy was in serious decline. Seeking a solution

▶

If you are a fan of Victorian architecture, plan to spend some time in Jim Thorpe.

Jim Thorpe, *cont.*

to their economic ills, the three towns banded together in 1954 taking the singular name of Jim Thorpe. The widow of the native American athlete had offered the name to any community that would develop a proper memorial. The united municipality built a mausoleum hoping to spark tourism in the area, but it wasn't until an early 1980s revitalization program spruced up the downtown area that tourists began returning to Jim Thorpe.

In recreation circles, Jim Thorpe is building a reputation as "the mountain bike capital of the east," spurred in part by the Switchback Trail and Lehigh Gorge State Park. With its friendly people, interesting shops, quaint bed-and-breakfasts and stunning Victorian architecture, Jim Thorpe should continue to attract a broad range of new visitors every year.

If you continue straight toward Summit Hill, you will soon pass a picnic table on your right, another pleasant setting for a short stop. The surface gets progressively more chunky as you head to Summit Hill, and the trail remains densely wooded. The one exception is about 1.5 miles from the former trestle, where a wide band of vegetation has been cleared to make way for the power lines overhead. Fortunately, this serves as a great overlook to the western end of Mauch Chunk Lake and the valley below.

During the month of October, the park sponsors hayrides on this section of the Switchback Trail, where fall colors radiate from every direction. Within another mile, you will enter the town of Summit Hill, where you will pass a convenience store and gas station. You can continue through town for a few blocks to Philip Ginder Park, where coal was discovered in 1791. From here, you can loop back through town, retrace your steps on the Switchback Trail and decide if you want to head up to Mount Pisgah.

To travel up to Mount Pisgah, where you can enjoy beautiful views of the Lehigh River and the surrounding gorge, take the sharp turn near the stone trestle remains. The vegetation in this area, which had initially been logged and then destroyed by fire in 1875,

is slowly making a comeback. In addition to oak, you may see occasional stands of white pine and hemlock. Rhododendron dominates the undergrowth, blooming in mid-summer.

You might also see some wildlife in the area, including black bear, wild turkey and porcupine. You will reach the trail's main obstacle about 2.5 miles from where you made the sharp turn. A portion of the corridor has eroded, so you need to cross a short, rocky ledge. If you have a bike, you will need to carry it.

Within 1.5 miles (steadily uphill), you will near the top of Mount Pisgah (elevation 1,400 feet), where you will initially get views of Jim Thorpe and then of the Lehigh River and the deep gorge. Before you reach the top, you will see a steep trail forking to the right. It is known as the "wagon road" and holds the key to your quick return to Jim Thorpe. Make a mental note of it before you go up to the summit and overlooks. When you get to the top, take some time to enjoy the views and catch your breath before heading down the wagon road.

With a grade topping 10 percent and a surface made of loose boulders and washed-out areas, the wagon road requires extreme caution, even on foot. If you do not consider yourself an advanced mountain bicyclist, seriously consider walking your bike down this half-mile descent.

Once you get to the bottom, turn left and then right onto Pine Street. Go one block and turn left onto Center Avenue. Proceed straight through the stop sign and use extra caution on the very steep half-mile-long descent. You will pass the Asa Packer Mansion, built by the founder of the Lehigh Valley Railroad, before descending into downtown Jim Thorpe.

Youghiogheny River Trail (North)

Endpoints: McKeesport to Connellsville

Location: Allegheny, Westmoreland and Fayette Counties

Length: 15.5 miles in three sections (will be 43 miles when complete)

Surface: Crushed limestone on developed sections; extremely large, chunky ballast on all undeveloped portions

Uses: 🚶 🚴 🏇 ♿ 🎣 ⛷

🚵 on undeveloped portions

Contact: Robert McKinley, Trail Manager
Regional Trail Corporation
P.O. Box 95
West Newton, PA 15089
412-872-5586

◆◆◆

When the non-profit Regional Trail Corporation formed in 1991, it could have had Dan Burnham's quote as its motto, "Make no small plans: they have no ability to stir men's souls." This group and scores of committed trail enthusiasts in western Pennsylvania have outlined a 315-mile trail network that could take trail users from downtown Pittsburgh to the heart of Washington, D.C. by the year 2000. And, the northern segment of the Youghiogheny River Trail is a key piece to completing the network.

Created in 1991 by Allegheny, Fayette and Westmoreland Counties, the Regional Trail Corporation was charged with acquiring, developing and managing the 43-mile Youghiogheny River Trail (North). The Youghiogheny River Trail (South) continues on the same

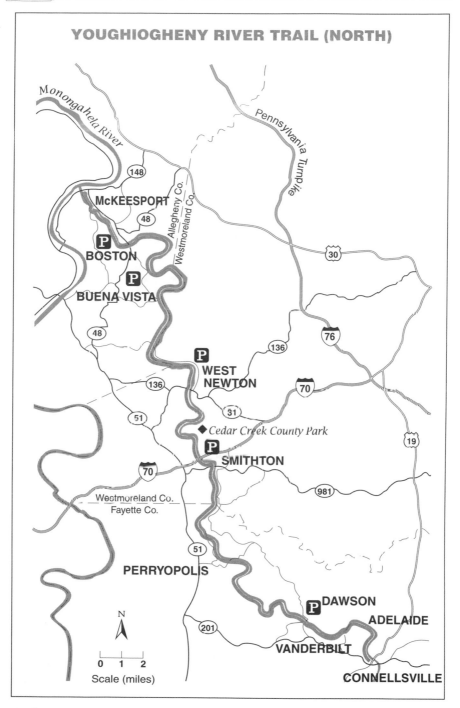

YOUGHIOGHENY RIVER TRAIL (NORTH)

corridor for another 27 miles below Connellsville and is managed by Ohiopyle State Park (see page 95).

Now that acquisition of the 43-mile corridor is complete, the Corporation is busy developing a high-quality recreation and transportation trail for the 200,000 people who live within five miles of the route. And, with nearly three million people living less than 90 minutes away, the trail could provide an economic boost to area businesses.

The trail originated in the early 1880s, when the Pittsburgh, McKeesport and Youghiogheny Railroad (nicknamed the "P-Mickey") built a new rail line to haul coal and coke to Pittsburgh's steel mills. Almost since the line's inception, the Pittsburgh and Lake Erie Railroad operated it. But use of the corridor declined when the steel industry fell on hard times, and P&LE filed to abandon the line in 1990. The trail has been under development ever since.

While only three sections of the Youghiogheny River Trail (North) have been developed, the entire corridor from Boston to just north of Connellsville is technically open. However, you should be aware that all undeveloped sections are extremely rugged, passable only by hikers and experienced mountain bicyclists. The surface consists of foot-deep, fist-sized chunks that once served as ballast for the railroad. Traveling on the undeveloped surface is at your own risk.

In developing the trail, the Regional Trail Corporation is refurbishing the original stone railroad mile markers, which began in downtown Pittsburgh. Therefore, the trail's current northern terminus is located at mile marker 19 in Boston's Riverfront Park.

Boston to Buena Vista

To reach the trail's northern terminus, take Pennsylvania State Route 48 north from Route 51. Just before crossing the Youghiogheny River in Boston, take a left onto West Smithfield and an immediate right onto Donner Street. The parking lot is located on the left side, virtually underneath the Route 48 bridge span.

The first 2.5 miles are a mix of wooded areas, private residences and some light industrial buildings. There are a few minor road crossings with minimal traffic. This is the newest section of trail, completed during summer 1994. The five miles south to Buena Vista opened in fall 1993.

Woods begin to embrace the trail by mile marker 22, creating a gorge-like setting. Near mile marker 23 a series of small waterfalls line the trail's right side. Meanwhile, the Youghiogheny River (pronounced yock-ah-GAIN-ee and affectionately referred to as "the Yough") darts in and out of view on the left. By mile marker 24, a common area for spotting wild turkey, the river views suddenly become more open.

Just before mile marker 25, you can take a break at the intriguing pre-Civil War Dravo Cemetery. From here, you can also follow a dirt road that leads to the river. The trail remains quite pleasant for the next couple of miles. An occasional stand of wildflowers adds to the impressive scenery. You will reach the town of Buena Vista before mile marker 27, approximately 7.5 miles from Boston.

NOTE: The next 6.5 miles, which feature some interesting relics of the coal-mining industry that once saturated the area, are undeveloped. The surface gets increasingly difficult south of Smithdale heading toward West Newton. This entire section of trail is slated for construction during the spring of 1995, so it may be

Karen-Lee Ryan

The views of the Youghiogheny Gorge are spectacular just a few miles south of Boston's Riverfront Park.

temporarily impassable while the surface is laid. Check with the trail manager for details.

West Newton to Smithton

The West Newton trailhead is located on the west bank of the Youghiogheny River, across the bridge from the downtown area. West Newton began as a pioneer stop in the late 1700s. Today, you will find a drugstore, several restaurants and a bike shop.

To reach the trail parking lot, take State Route 136 east from Route 51; the lot is on the right side just before the bridge crossing. A kiosk in the parking lot usually features a current trail map, indicating which sections are under development.

As you begin this section, the river is quite close to the trail on the left. You will see a small cemetery on the right soon after you leave the parking lot. Before long, shelves of rock rise above you along the trail's right side. Some of the best river views appear before you as you ease around a bend just before mile marker 34.

Sitting alongside the trail just ahead is an old railroad passenger car that the Regional Trail Corporation would like to convert to a trail headquarters someday. The next relic of the trail's origins is an abandoned coal mine and coal cleaning plant. You will also see several coal-waste piles, known in this area as "gob piles."

Soon more shelves of rock reclaim the trail's right side, and the magnificent river views return. If you look closely at the rocks, you will see some interesting patterns, which were created when the rocks were under water thousands of years ago. An occasional trickle of waterfall is the only water these rocks see today.

About 3.5 miles from West Newton, you will reach pristine Cedar Creek County Park, which features numerous picnic tables, grills, restrooms, drinking water, a boat launch and two extensive parking areas. You can also venture onto the Cedar Creek Gorge Trail—a great place to enjoy wildflowers. The developed portion of trail ends four miles from West Newton at the edge of the park.

The next two miles leading to Smithton are not developed. And while the surface is chunky, the trail is passable on foot or on a sturdy mountain bike. On this section of trail you might hear an occasional whistle from the active rail line on the river's other bank. It adds to the rustic feeling of this area.

At about 38.5 miles, you will cross under the massive span

of Interstate 70. From there, the trail surface deteriorates rapidly. You'll find many pools of water amid the large chunks of ballast. Fortunately, the Smithton access area—a popular destination for anglers—is less than a mile away.

NOTE: The next 13.5 miles of undeveloped trail from Smithton to Dawson are by far the most rugged and remote of the entire trail. There are few homes or road crossings and no alternate routes for the majority of the distance. The trail surface is worse than any other section of trail with many pools of water and washouts along the way. And if that is isn't warning enough that traveling this section requires some serious planning, be aware that copperheads are commonplace in some areas along this section.

Dawson to Adelaide

This 2.4-mile section is the only part of the trail open in Fayette County. You can reach the trail from State Route 219 just prior to the bridge crossing east into Dawson, a wonderful hamlet with beautiful Victorian architecture. Once you are on the trail west of Dawson, you will be approximately at the trail's 53-mile mark. The river views here are wide open and pleasant.

Between miles 53.5 and 54.5 are a series of century-old beehive coke ovens in the hillside west of the trail. In another half mile you will reach the end of the surfaced section at Adelaide. A campground is located here, where you can get soft drinks and other refreshments in the camp store. Hikers, bicyclists and equestrians are welcome.

The last three miles may be inaccessible during part of 1995 as coal mining will be taking place in the trail's vicinity. South of that section, two extensive bridge spans in Connellsville need to have decking and handrails built before they can be opened to trail users. The state plans to develop these during mid-1995. At the same time, many of the undeveloped sections of the Youghiogheny River Trail (North) could be under construction.

Once these remote sections are developed and these bridges are open for trail users, a direct connection will be made to the Youghiogheny River Trail (South). It currently begins in Confluence and runs north through Ohiopyle State Park to the undeveloped bridges in Connellsville (see next page for details). When connected together, they will form a spectacular—and lengthy—trail along the scenic Youghiogheny River.

Youghiogheny River Trail (South)

Endpoints: Confluence to Connellsville

Location: Fayette and Somerset Counties

Length: 24 miles

Surface: hard-packed crushed limestone

Uses:

Contact: Douglas Hoehn, Park Superintendent
Ohiopyle State Park
P.O. Box 105
Ohiopyle, PA 15470
412-329-8591

◆◆◆

I f you want to get away from the stresses of urban and
suburban living, the southern section of the Youghiogheny River
Trail offers a beautifully remote setting. Only two small towns
and a handful of road crossings break up the spectacular scenery
of the densely wooded corridor nestled alongside the breathtaking
Youghiogheny River. Of course, a few hundred thousand other trail
lovers have already discovered this idyllic route, so don't expect to
enjoy the area alone.

The Youghiogheny River (pronounced yock-ah-GAIN-ee, and
typically called "the Yough") has attracted vast numbers of family-
oriented whitewater rafters for years. And the 18,719-acre Ohiopyle
State Park, with 223 campsites and dozens of miles of hiking trails,
now attracts more than three million people annually. The park
surrounds much of the rail-trail, which is adding yet another
dimension to an extremely popular recreation area.

Ohiopyle was a flourishing town—with sawmills, gristmills,
quarries, tanneries and a barrel making factory when the railroads

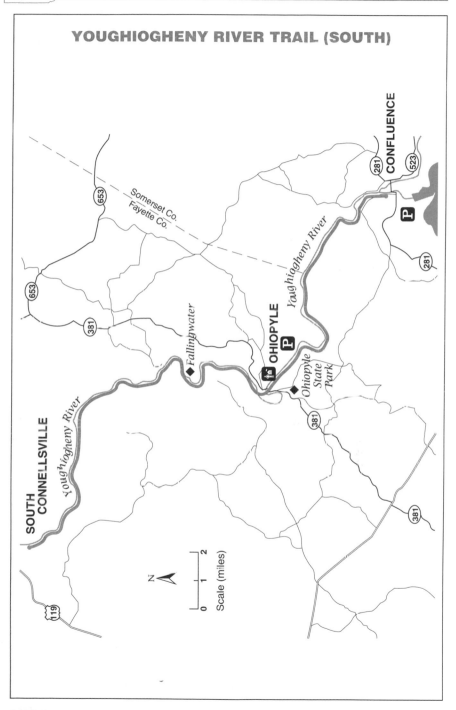

YOUGHIOGHENY RIVER TRAIL (SOUTH)

came to the surrounding area in the late 1800s. By the early 1900s, coal mining and coke production were the town's primary industries. In 1910, the Western Maryland Railroad began building a line through Ohiopyle, which was eventually abandoned in 1960. Acquisition of the state park land and much of the rail corridor began in the mid-1960s. The first 10 miles of trail opened in 1986, and the 14 additional miles south of Connellsville opened in the early 1990s.

To reach the trail's southern access point near Confluence, head south on State Route 281 through Confluence; cross the one-lane bridge over the Youghiogheny and into Fayette County. Take a sharp right onto Ram Cat Hollow Road, which parallels the river. You will travel nearly two miles on this road before reaching the trail's parking lot, where restrooms are located. Take a left onto the trail to head toward Ohiopyle. If you go right, you will basically retrace your steps back to Confluence.

Once on the trail, you are instantly in the woods, with the river below on the right side and a steep embankment of trees off to the left. You will pass mile marker 2 within a half-mile. Below you is

The "High Bridge" over the Youghiogheny River leads backpackers to several hiking trails throughout Ohiopyle State Park.

excellent whitewater, where kayakers and canoers often negotiate a gated course.

For the next few miles, the trees on the trail's left side gracefully arch over the trail and occasionally yield to patches of rocky escarpments. Waterfalls sporadically trickle into a wild-fern groundcover. By mile marker 5, the views open up to the landscapes on both sides of the trail—you will see mountainous terrain off to the left and the meandering path of the Yough on the right. A number of benches and pull-off areas have been created for you to take advantage of the beauty around you. The largest pull-off area is located just before mile marker 6.

If you look closely, you may see some relics of the industries that once operated in the area. Foundations from an old stone quarry are located near mile marker 5, and a stone fence from a former farm is at approximately 6.3 miles. The river weaves in and out of view for the next couple of miles, although the scenery remains spectacular throughout. You might catch a glimpse of a few railroad remnants near mile marker 9, just a mile shy of Ohiopyle.

Beyond 9.5, you will pass alongside the first of two large trail parking areas, which are often full on weekends. By mile marker 10 you will find the visitors' center. Located in an old train station, the center offers information about local history and displays photographs that document the area's past. In addition, you can find additional information on what to do in the area. Restrooms are also located in the building.

The town of Ohiopyle is worth an excursion off the trail. Several restaurants, an ice cream parlor, craft shops, a book store and a growing number of amenities are all geared toward recreationists. You can also view the Ohiopyle Falls, take a swim, visits several hiking trails or play softball or volleyball—all within a couple of blocks of the trail. And, if you want to run some rapids, several rafting outfitters are located in town.

To continue north on the trail toward Connellsville, cut through the trail parking lot, take a right on the paved road and go about a block. Take another right to cross a bridge over the Youghiogheny River and take a left on the other side into another trail parking lot. This is also the access point for the Ferncliff Natural Area and several hiking trails.

Tom Sexton

You will typically see many whitewater rafters along the southern
section of the Youghiogheny River Trail.

Almost immediately after getting onto the trail—less than a half-mile from the visitors' center—you will cross the "High Bridge." The view from the bridge is easily the most spectacular of the entire trail. In summer months, dozens of gawking visitors often line the bridge and photograph rafters below. You can get to the Great Gorge Hiking Trail just beyond the bridge on the left side.

The next 14 miles of trail can only be described as magnificent. In fact, this section of trail may have influenced editors of *Travel and Leisure* magazine to hail the Youghiogheny River Trail as "one of the 18 great walks in the world" in a 1994 issue. And there is nothing to break up the consistently breathtaking scenery—no amenities, no towns, no major road crossings. As one local trail enthusiast said, "It all looks the same: it's so beautiful, you can barely stand it."

You will typically see many rafters along the way, and a number of benches and pull-off areas allow you to watch them for as long as you like. Near mile marker 13 you may be able to see rafters tackle such rapids as Dimple Rock, Swimmers Rapid and Bottle of Wine Rapid. Two hiking trails cross the Youghiogheny River Trail between mile markers 13 and 14. A wall of rocks lines the trail at this point, which has been the site of an occasional rock slide.

The rafters' take out point is located near mile marker 16, where you will cross a small road used by the rafting outfitters. Prior to mile marker 17, you will pass the Rock Run Creek and Falls on the left. In late spring and summer, the vegetation may obscure the view of the creek and falls, but you can see them by venturing a short distance into the woods. Beyond mile marker 19, you will see a few huts and a building, all part of the Camp Carmel Baptist Camp.

Between miles 20 and 24, several short paths lead to the river, where you may want to dip your toes or relax in the sun. Several benches are also scattered along the trail. Steep walls of rock occasionally break up the wooded views on the left, while the river comes in and out of view on the right.

At mile marker 24, you have reached an area known as Wheeler Bottom. A water treatment plant on the trail's right side signals the end of the developed portion of the trail. You will also see "Trail Closed" signs. Up a short distance is a maze of rail corridors and bridges that once sliced through Connellsville. Two massive bridges need extensive decking and handrails before they can be opened

The Youghiogheny River Trail South cuts through Ohiopyle State Park, a popular family destination.

for trail use. While work on the bridges was delayed in 1994, the state plans to open them in 1995.

When this southern section of the Youghiogheny River Trail is complete, it will link to the Yough's northern section (see page 89) to create a dynamic and continuous 70-mile rail-trail.

Future plans call for the Youghiogheny River Trail to connect to the Allegheny Highlands Trail (see page 14), which will soon link to the 180-mile towpath of the C&O Canal National Historical Park that leads directly into Washington, D.C.

An Introduction to Rail-Trails in New Jersey

As with other states in the Mid-Atlantic, the railroad was an integral part of New Jersey's history. In 1918, New Jersey was home to nearly 2,500 miles of active railroad corridor. Today, less than half remain active.

To expedite the process of preserving railroad corridors and converting them into trails, various trail users got together in the early 1990s to form an advocacy group known as New Jersey Rail-Trails. This group is providing a voice for rail-trails throughout the state, while several other local trail groups help fuel the movement.

Across the state, 18 rail corridors totaling nearly 150 miles, have been recycled into multi-use trails. And, another 13 projects are underway.

Although local opposition has stalled a number of New Jersey rail-trail projects, the future is looking brighter. After more than a decade, the Paulinskill Valley Trail has finally opened under the management of the state park system. This success stems in large part from the determination of the citizen-run Paulinskill Valley Trail Association. The obstacles they have overcome may help other trails open in significantly less time.

The three New Jersey rail-trails highlighted in this book are excellent examples of the variety the Garden State has to offer. From restored canal locks to bayfront communities to rural countrysides, the rail-trails of New Jersey offer fun and interesting places to explore.

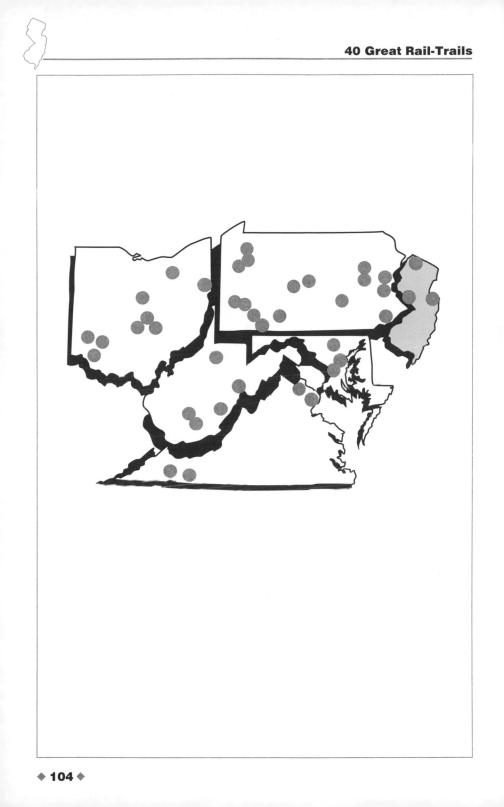

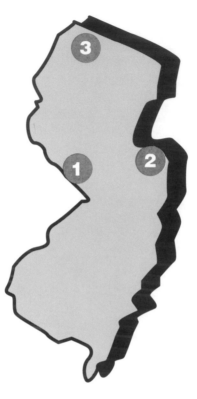

NEW JERSEY'S GREAT RAIL-TRAILS

1. Delaware & Raritan Canal State Park
2. Henry Hudson Trail
3. Paulinskill Valley Trail

The Prallsville Mills near Stockton are among the many structures
preserved along the canal.

Delaware and Raritan Canal State Park

Endpoints: Frenchtown to Trenton and Trenton to New Brunswick

Location: Hunterdon, Mercer and Somerset Counties

Length: 32 miles of a 68-mile trail are on abandoned rail corridor

Surface: packed crushed stone and gravel, ranging from hard-packed to loose

Uses:  on certain sections

Contact: Paul Stern, Superintendent
Delaware and Raritan Canal State Park
625 Canal Road
Somerset, NJ 08873
908-873-3050

◆◆◆

The Delaware and Raritan Canal State Park beautifully preserves two historic forms of transportation—canals and railroads—while connecting the state capital with rural and suburban areas of central New Jersey. With the park's close proximity to several major cities, it's no surprise that more than a half-million people explore this significant historic facility that has gained new life as a multi-use recreational trail.

In 1834, the 44-mile main channel of the Delaware and Raritan Canal between Bordentown and New Brunswick opened with great fanfare as previously isolated central New Jerseyans celebrated

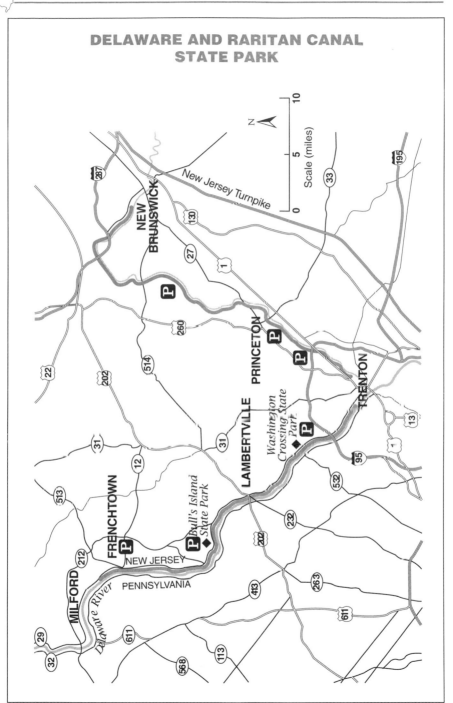

DELAWARE AND RARITAN CANAL STATE PARK

their connection to the rest of the world. The canal, dug by hand by Irish immigrants, used a series of 14 canal locks to transport coal from Philadelphia to New York City. To supply the canal with water, a 22-mile feeder channel was built along the Delaware River between Trenton and Milford. This "feeder canal" quickly became a busy navigation channel as well.

In 1851 the Belvidere-Delaware Railroad was built along the feeder canal. The canal became one of America's most important and active waterways. Its busiest years were the decade that followed the Civil War. In the late 1800s, the Pennsylvania Railroad took over both the canal and the railroad. The railroad proved more economical than the canal, and after nearly 100 years, the D&R Canal ceased operation in 1933. It was outlasted by the thriving Pennsylvania Railroad, although by the early 1970s, the railroad had gone the same way as the canal.

Over the years the state had maintained the canal, operating it as a source of water for nearby farms, industry and homes. In 1973, the entire canal route was added to the National Register of Historic Places, and it was designated a state park in 1974.

Today the canal forms a "V" through the waist of New Jersey, with Trenton as the southernmost point. The western leg between Milford and Trenton along the Delaware River has been developed (and surfaced with crushed stone) on the former rail line adjacent to the canal. The trail's eastern leg between Trenton and New Brunswick exists on the original towpath of the main canal, and its surface is more rugged. Unfortunately, a portion of the canal in the urbanized Trenton area has been filled in and is not accessible to trail users. Therefore, you may want to consider touring the Delaware and Raritan Canal over two (or more) days.

Frenchtown to Trenton

The easiest place to gain access to the northern end of the D&R Canal is the quaint town of Frenchtown, located on the Delaware River about 13 miles southeast of Interstate 78 via Route 513. The trail and canal cut through the heart of town, which abounds with bed-and-breakfasts, antique shops and restaurants. You can park adjacent to the trail where it intersects Bridge Street. From Frenchtown, you can travel north on the trail two miles to its terminus

south of Milford, where the railroad tracks resume. If you head south, you can travel more than 30 miles through small towns and rural landscapes, visiting many historic structures and two sizable state parks along the way.

The trail is arrow straight and lined with a thin band of trees as you head south. Initially you will pass a few residences, and within a mile you traverse the Kingswood access area. It offers a boat launch and additional parking adjacent to State Route 29. For the next several miles, the trail closely parallels Route 29, although the expansive Delaware River views will divert your attention from the steady flow of traffic. The trail continues flat and straight, veiled by slender trees on both sides. Take some time to look around, and you will realize that you are near the base of a gorge carved by the Delaware River over many years.

More than eight miles from Frenchtown, you will notice a cluster of houses sandwiched between the trail and the river. Another boat launch is located in the area, as is parking for a few cars. Within another mile, you will be in Bull's Island State Park, which offers more than 80 campsites, dozens of picnic tables and grills, a nature trail, bathrooms, telephones and extensive parking. From

The area south of Lambertville is often heavily used.

this 24-acre park, which is a nesting area for several warblers, you also can take a pedestrian bridge over the Delaware River into Pennsylvania.

For the next two miles, dense woods block views to the river, and the trail closely parallels Route 29. A large outcropping of rocks diverts the road away from the trail just before you reach the historic Prallsville Mills near the town of Stockton. You cannot miss the old structures that have been lovingly restored in recent years. Among the buildings, which were serviced by the canal and railroad, are a wooden grist mill dating back to 1711, a stone linseed oil mill from 1790, a grain silo and a feed storage building. One of the canal's locks has also been restored in this area, where parking is available.

As soon as you leave the Prallsville Mills area, you will enter the town of Stockton, where several cafes and shops have opened in stunning Victorian buildings. In about 2.5 miles, you will pass under U.S. Route 202 before heading into the Lambertville.

This Victorian-era community bustles with shops, restaurants, bed-and-breakfasts, inns and interesting architecture—not to mention tourists. The town is one of five nationally-registered historic communities along the trail. It marks the approximate mid-point of the feeder canal and warrants a visit. And, if Lambertville doesn't satisfy your appetite for quaint shops and restaurants, take Bridge Street (which prohibits bicycles) across the Delaware River and into New Hope, Pennsylvania. Another tourist attraction, New Hope offers even more shops, restaurants and inns.

As you head out of Lambertville, the river becomes significantly wider. The views are excellent despite some trees lining the trail and canal. Within another 1.5 miles, a tract of land—apparently used for hay farming—suddenly separates the trail from the river. Before long, the river reappears before woods hinder the views again. You will pass through the small town of Titusville before reaching Washington Crossing State Park.

Here, General George Washington crossed the Delaware River to attack British soldiers in Trenton on Christmas night in 1776. Today, this large park offers picnicking, extensive parking, benches, interpretive signs and bathrooms adjacent to the trail. A few original structures from the 1700s are also located here.

Continuing south, the trail begins to take on a more suburban

feel. In nearly 2.5 miles you will pass Scudders Falls before going under State Route 29 and Interstate 95. At this point, the trail veers away from the river and cuts through attractive suburbs of Trenton. The canal and trail are serenely isolated from traffic except for a few road crossings. First you will cross Upper Ferry Road, followed by Lower Ferry Road about a mile later. After passing a golf course, you will cross over Sullivan Trail Road on a former railroad bridge as the trail gets progressively more urban.

This section of the Delaware and Raritan Canal State Park ends at Prospect Road in Trenton.

Trenton to New Brunswick

The southernmost access point on the main canal is at Mulberry Street in Trenton. To reach it, take Interstate 95 north from Philadelphia to U.S. Route 1 north. Cross over the Delaware River into Trenton, and take the Mulberry Street exit. The trail and canal begin one block west of the highway. Parking in this very urban area is extremely limited.

The first three miles of trail, which pass through primarily commercial and industrial areas, are surfaced. However, the subsequent three miles present many obstacles, including a detour of U.S. Route 1. With these difficulties in mind, many people start near Port Mercer. To get there, take Province Line Road west from Route 1 (at Mercer Mall). Cross over Route 1 and travel about a half mile, passing the Port Mercer Canal House. Turn right onto Mercer County Route 533 and turn right again into a small dirt parking lot in 0.3 miles. From this point, you can follow the canal and trail northeast for nearly 30 miles to New Brunswick.

The trail assumes a surprisingly rural tone at this point, even though heavily developed Route 1 is only about a mile away. Across from the parking lot, you will see farmland and old homesteads. The trail, with its hard-packed dirt and gravel surface, is surrounded by trees on either side. This peaceful stretch of trail is heavily used, especially on weekends.

Within about 2.5 miles, you will reach the outskirts of Princeton, the attractive Ivy League college town. At Alexander Road, a nature preserve has been developed with restrooms, picnic tables, shelters, a playground and extensive parking. You can also rent

canoes here. In the mid-1800s this area, known as Princeton Basin, was a small community with a hotel and several saloons catering to canal and railroad workers.

If you head west (left) onto Alexander Road, you can follow a bike route adjacent to the road for about a mile to University Place.

Wilma Frey

You will see many restored canal locks along this trail.

Wilma Frey

The Delaware & Raritan Canal offers a quiet, wooded setting.

If you turn right here, you will pass by several campus buildings before arriving in the heart of picturesque Princeton. This short jaunt is worth a side-trip, especially if you are interested in browsing through some shops and looking at Colonial-style architecture. You will also find a wide variety of cafes, restaurants and coffee shops.

The next town, geared toward trail users, is Kingston—less than four miles from Princeton via the D&R Canal. Here, near the State Route 27 underpass, you will find a couple of gift shops and several restaurants as well as parking. The Kingston Lock has been restored here, and it is an interesting feature to view. The Millstone River also begins paralleling the canal in this area, and you can rent a canoe for use on either waterway. Two boat launches are provided.

As you head toward the tiny town of Rocky Hill, which was founded in 1760, the trail becomes progressively more rural. While there are no trail-related amenities here, parking is available. You will cross County Road 518 at grade and before returning to the wooded corridor.

The next eight miles are the most remote section of trail, and they are straight and mostly wooded. About 2.5 miles from Rocky Hill, you will pass the Griggstown Lock, followed soon after by a small day-use area with parking and canoe rentals. The tunnel of trees that encompasses the trail continues beyond the Griggstown area. In another 3.5 miles, you will approach the town of Blackwells Mill, where you will find a restored canal house and a park setting with picnic tables and parking. The Delaware and Raritan Canal State Park offices are located nearby on Canal Road, where you can also see some interesting architecture.

In another two miles you will enter the town of East Millstone, where a small park offers basketball courts and a playground. Nearby, you will find several stunning Victorian homes, although there are no trail-related facilities. You will cross Amwell Road (County Road 514) at grade.

From this point, the surrounding landscape begins to get more developed over the next few miles, with residential areas mixed with light industrial and commercial establishments. As you head into Bound Brook after passing under Interstate 287, industrial buildings and warehouses dominate the area. This wanes, however,

as the canal and trail bend southeast toward New Brunswick. You can enter Bound Brook via Main Street, where you will find several cafes and a diner.

Outside of Bound Brook, the trail runs mostly parallel to Easton Avenue, home to fast food restaurants and strip malls. Fortunately, the trail and canal remain surprisingly isolated and peaceful, highlighting the significance of this state park that has secured critical open space in a rapidly developing area.

About two miles from the trail's terminus, you will pass through an area known as Bogan's Meadows, where the historic Van Wizkle House is a popular tourist attraction. The trail ends at the Landing Lane Bridge, near the edge of New Brunswick. From here, you are close to Rutgers University and the Raritan Bay.

Henry Hudson Trail

Endpoints: Aberdeen Township to Leonardo

Location: Monmouth County

Length: 9 miles

Surface: Packed gravel and dirt

Uses: 🚶 🚴 🐎 ♿

Contact: Monmouth County Park System
Public Information Office
805 Newman Springs Road
Lincroft, NJ 07738-1695
908-842-4000

◆◆◆

The Henry Hudson Trail offers plenty of scenic diversity as it traverses several small towns, some wetlands and a creek. The trail also provides opportunities to explore intriguing museums, historic bayfront communities, a haunted house, an amusement park and the Sandy Hook Gateway National Recreation Area.

Until passenger and freight service stopped in 1966, the Bayshore Line of the Central Railroad of New Jersey was a folksy commuter line serving eight towns along the Raritan Bay: Aberdeen, Keyport, Union Beach, Keansburg, Port Monmouth, Belford, Leonardo and Atlantic Highlands. The corridor now serves the communities in a different way—as a multi-use trail.

The trailhead is located in Aberdeen. To get there from the north, take Interstate 287, the New Jersey Turnpike or Route 440 to the Garden State Parkway south. From the Parkway, take the Aberdeen Exit (#117-A) and turn left onto Lloyd Road. In 0.2 miles, you will find about a dozen parking spaces for the trail at Gerard Avenue.

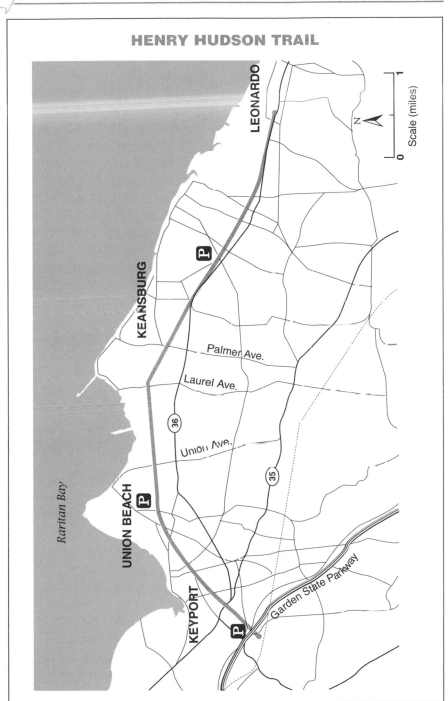

HENRY HUDSON TRAIL

LEONARDO

Scale (miles)

N

KEANSBURG

Palmer Ave.

Laurel Ave.

36

Union Ave.

35

Raritan Bay

UNION BEACH

Garden State Parkway

KEYPORT

Brian Schmult

The Henry Hudson Trail cuts through several small communities.

To reach the trailhead from the south, take the Garden State Parkway north to exit 117 (Keyport). Beyond the tollbooth, turn right onto Clark Street, and then take the second right onto Beers Street and go one mile. Next, turn right on Church Street and proceed one mile to Lloyd Road. In 1.3 miles, you will find parking at Gerard Avenue.

From the trailhead in Aberdeen, you will travel through a residential area of Keyport for the first three-quarters of a mile to Broad Street. This town was once an important oyster processing and exporting site that served the New York markets via steamboat.

The Marie Cottrell playground now occupies the site of the former Keyport Station. At this point, you can take a 1.5-mile loop side trip to see the Steamboat Dock Museum and the grand, Victorian architecture of Keyport. First, travel a half-mile north on Broad Street to the museum; then go east for almost a mile on First Street, where you will see Keyport's Victorian homes. At the the fork, veer right onto Stone Street, where you can get back on the Henry Hudson trail just beyond the steel street bridge over Chingarora Creek.

The next two miles take you through Union Beach, where pottery and bricks were once manufactured. The Henry Hudson Trail crosses Natco Lake, one of the largest and most intact wetlands along the entire Bayshore. If you smell a perfumy aroma in this area, it probably comes from a nearby fragrance factory.

Approximately 3.5 miles from the Aberdeen trailhead, the trail passes through Keansburg, where you can take another side trip—this time to the Keansburg bayfront. If you go north on Laurel Avenue toward the Beachway, you will reach a beach and an amusement park in less than a mile. In its heyday, Keansburg boomed with hotels and boarding houses. Today it is reemerging as a beachfront tourist attraction.

About a half-mile after crossing Laurel Avenue, you will reach Wilson Avenue. Here, you will find the only station still standing on this former Central Railroad of New Jersey line. Plans call for converting a caboose that sits on a section of track into a train museum next to the station.

For another interesting side trip from the trail, you can take Wilson Avenue one mile north to the Spy House Museum. Said to be haunted, the Whitlock-Seabrook-Wilson House began as a private residence in 1676.

Continuing on the Henry Hudson Trail, you will soon cross Compton's Creek and enter Belford. This town is home to the Belford Seafood Cooperative, the Bayshore's largest shellfish processing plant. Here in 1900, J. Howard Smith perfected a way to extract oil from inedible menhaden fish. The oil has been widely used in cosmetics and pharmaceuticals.

The United States Navy's Earle Naval Weapons Station is also located in this area between Belford and Leonardo. The station's 2.5-mile pier can service up to five ammunition supply ships at once.

The trail ends one mile beyond this point in Leonardo. Even though the trail ends, you are close to two other attractions. At the Sandy Hook Gateway National Recreation Area you can swim and hike. At the Twin Lights Historical Site, you can tour the two lighthouses, built in 1862, and the museum. Both attractions are approximately five miles away via State Route 36.

Paulinskill Valley Trail

Endpoints: Brugler Road near Columbia to Sparta Junction

Location: Warren and Sussex Counties

Length: 26 miles

Surface: Cinder

Uses: 🚶 🚴 🐎 🎣 ⛷️

Contact: Rocky Gott, Park Superintendent
Kittatinny Valley State Park
P.O. Box 621
Andover, NJ 07821
201-786-6445

Len Frank, President
Paulinskill Valley Trail Committee
P.O. Box 7076
Hackettstown, NJ 07840
908-852-0587

◆◆◆

T he Paulinskill Valley Trail leads you through farm fields, rolling hills, woods and swamps. Along the way, you can see nearly one quarter of New Jersey's plant species. And, the newest state park rail-trail offers spectacular views of the rural northwestern New Jersey countryside. All this, while paralleling the scenic Paulinskill River.

The Paulinskill Valley Trail takes its roots from the New York, Susquehanna and Western Railroad (NYS&W). John I. Blair, once the richest man in New Jersey, started building the first railroad through the Paulinskill Valley from Blairstown (his namesake) to

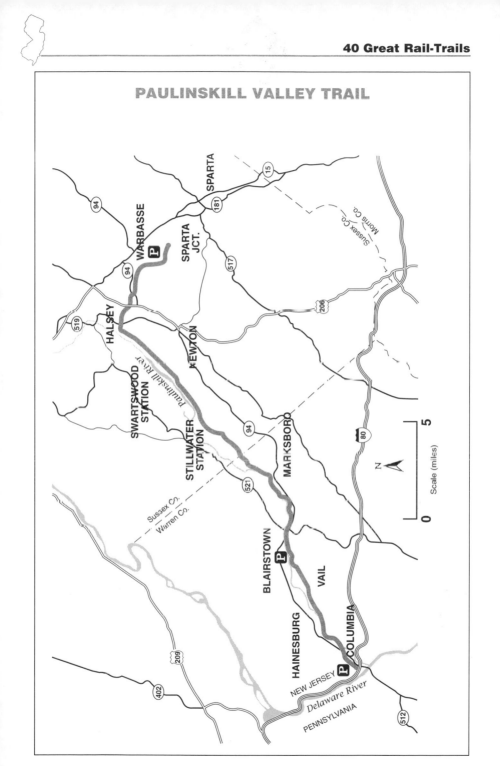

PAULINSKILL VALLEY TRAIL

the Delaware River at Delaware in 1876. He sold the corridor to NYS&W within five years. In 1882, New York Susquehanna and Western extended the rail line west up the valley and east to Jersey City. The purpose of this new railroad was to bring coal—mined in northeastern Pennsylvania—to New York City.

Creameries began to sprout up alongside many stations on the railroad, which soon hauled a variety of dairy products. Later the Lehigh and New England Railroad shared more than 18.5 miles of corridor with NYS&W to transport coal to New England. In 1962 the rail line was abandoned. The rails and ties were removed, and the City of Newark bought the corridor. After years of urging by the volunteer-run Paulinskill Valley Trail Committee, the State purchased the corridor in 1992 and began converting it into a trail. Trail-related improvements, including decking and handrails on bridges, should be completed by the end of 1995.

It is easiest to reach the rural and somewhat rugged Paulinskill Valley Trail on its western end, at the stone arch bridge on Brugler Road, which is located on the National Historic Register. From Columbia, on the Delaware River just south of the Delaware Water

The relatively rugged Paulinskill Valley Trail traverses rural northwestern New Jersey.

Gap, take State Route 94 north about one mile to Brugler Road. Turn right to cross the bridge that leads to the trailhead.

Along the route, watch for preserved relics from the corridor's past: mileage markers, whistleposts, cattle crossings, battery boxes and signal stands. The trail follows the Paulinskill River up the valley through woods and lush fields. Beyond the first mile, a cinder path leads you past a battery box to Hainesburg Junction, where the Lehigh and New England Railroad originally joined in from the left (the two railroads shared the one corridor for many years between here and Swartswood Junction). You will see the railroad's only remaining building, known as a wheel knocking shed, on your left. From here, railroad workers inspected the trains before they continued on the corridor.

Soon you will pass mile post 89, which still accurately indicates that you are 89 miles from Jersey City. Several original mile markers exist along the route to help you gage your distance. From here you can see the spectacular Hainesburg Viaduct, a concrete arched structure that was considered the eighth wonder of the world when it was completed in 1911. Towering 115 feet high and stretching 1,100 feet long, this Delaware, Lackawanna and Western Railroad's "cutoff" over the Paulinskill Valley was once the largest concrete structure in the world. Known as the "Lackawanna Cutoff," this nine-arch viaduct cut off more than 11 miles of steeply graded rail corridor in the valley.

When you get to the Station Road intersection, turn left and continue under the viaduct. Just east of the structure are the remains of Hainesburg Station and a turntable (where engines were turned around to pull the train in the opposite direction). A creamery was once located to the west. Today, parking is available for horse trailers in this area. Continue along Station Road and bear right into the woods before the road crosses the Paulinskill River. Station Road meets State Route 94 on the other side.

A power line crosses the trail providing a view of Kittatinny Mountain (also known as Blue Mountain) to the west. Cross your first bridge near Crisman Road, where the original mile marker 87 may be obscured. Soon you will find yourself passing farm fields and a farmstead on your left.

Next, you will cross Vail Road, where you can see an old creamery and feed store on the right. On the side of the building, you

will notice the high doors that were used by rail cars. The trail continues through a cut, and then over an area filled in by the railroad. Near the Gwinnup Road intersection, you may notice a post with a "W" on it. Known as a whistlepost, this alerted train engineers to blow their whistles to warn of the train's approach. (This whistlepost has been moved from its original location, which was some distance from the intersection.)

The trail bears left and follows a tree-lined corridor through fields to Blairstown Airport, where you will need to take a minor detour. Keep a lookout for aircraft, and take the taxiway and road to your right. Continue around the hangar and snack bar to Lambert Road. Turn left and follow Lambert to the end of the airport runway. The Paulinskill Valley Trail continues to your right through the woods. Here you may see mileage marker 84, which means you have come about five miles from the Hainesburg Viaduct.

Soon you will skirt a series of horse exercise rings on your left. The next mile of trail was once used to train thoroughbred race horses. The Paulinskill River joins the trail again at Footbridge Park in Blairstown, where plenty of parking is available. This area once bustled with Blairstown Station, a creamery, coal chutes, a turntable and a lumberyard. The historic footbridge leads into town, where you will find a couple of places to eat.

Over the next four miles, the trail crosses the Paulinskill River four times. The bridge decking is scheduled for completion by fall 1995. The Paulins Dam, a local fishing spot with parking, is located on the right beyond the first bridge. After the second bridge, the trail heads into the woods. After the third bridge—the trail's highest—the trail intersects with Spring Valley Road at Marksboro, where parking is available. You may see an original road crossing signal box as you continue one mile to the final bridge.

After you cross a grassy area, look for a concrete culvert crossing a small stream. In the 1950s, a flash flood blocked this culvert and undermined the tracks, causing a freight train to derail. A truck from one of the derailed railroad cars can be seen at the edge of the field further down on your left.

You will pass into Sussex County near the trail's mid-point. Beyond a railroad signal stand and a pond is Water Wheel Horse Farm, the site of the golden spike ceremony the day after the trail was acquired in 1992. Next, you will pass a horse barn, cross Wall

Street, and continue on to Stillwater Station Road and a creamery.

The next crossing will be County Route 610, and soon you will pass another creamery. After crossing Kohlbocker Road, you will need to take a small detour. Just before Paulinskill Lake Road follow the path to the left up the embankment onto Kohlbocker Road. Cross Paulinskill Lake Road and continue on South Shore Drive. The trail immediately resumes on your right and remains elevated along the east side of Paulinskill Lake. A few rock cuts and fills and the remains of Swartswood Creamery appear on the left. Bear left past the Swartswood Station foundation and cross Swartswood Road, County Route 622. Scramble up the embankment and continue to Swartswood Junction.

Swartswood Junction, nearly 20 miles from your starting point, is where the Lehigh and New England line originally branched off to the left. Stay to the right, and soon after you pass a cattle crossing, you will see a waterfall on the right. After you cross Plotts Road, you can enjoy a view of the Sussex County landscape, thanks to an opening created by a power line corridor.

As you enter Halsey, the trail sweeps right through a limestone cut and over another area filled in by the railroad. In a short distance, you will cross County Route 519, traversing farm fields on the right and a pond on the left.

You can bypass a deep—and typically wet—cut between U.S. Route 206 and State Route 94 by following Sid Taylor Road to State Route 94. Here, scramble up the embankment, continue past rock cliffs on the left and commercial peat mining on the right. This is an excellent birding area.

Soon you will cross the Paulinskill River. Proceed to Warbasse Junction, which has parking for horse trailers. Beyond Warbasse Junction Road, the Sussex Branch Trail—a 20 mile rail-trail that forms part of Kittatinny Valley State Park—crosses the Paulinskill Valley Trail, which continues for a short distance through woodlands.

The trail's eastern terminus is about one mile from Garrison Road. Parking is available at Garrison Road, which serves as the current eastern trailhead. The last mile of the Paulinskill Valley Trail crosses a swampy area and continues over a foot bridge before ending at Sparta Junction. Here, the New York, Susquehanna and Western Railroad remains active, so no trail access is possible.

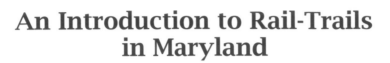

An Introduction to Rail-Trails in Maryland

In Maryland, it's quality not quantity that counts when it comes to rail-trails.

While Maryland has completed just seven rail-trails totaling less than 50 miles, they are of exceptional quality and serve as models for the rest of the state and the nation. And, the 20 rail-trail projects in the works promise to add new dimensions to the state's growing network of trails.

The state of Maryland has a long railroad history. In fact, the Baltimore and Ohio Railroad was the nation's first, opening in 1827. Despite its bold beginnings, the railroad industry in Maryland has been dwindling for most of this century.

Fortunately, agencies at the local, county and state level—working with numerous rail-trail advocates—are preserving some of Maryland's railroad history. Throughout the state, a number of former rail lines are gaining new life as recreation and transportation trails.

The three Maryland rail-trails highlighted in this book are excellent examples of the variety Maryland has to offer. From urban Washington, D.C., to suburban Baltimore to the rural environs just south of the Mason-Dixon Line, the rail-trails of Maryland are well worth a visit!

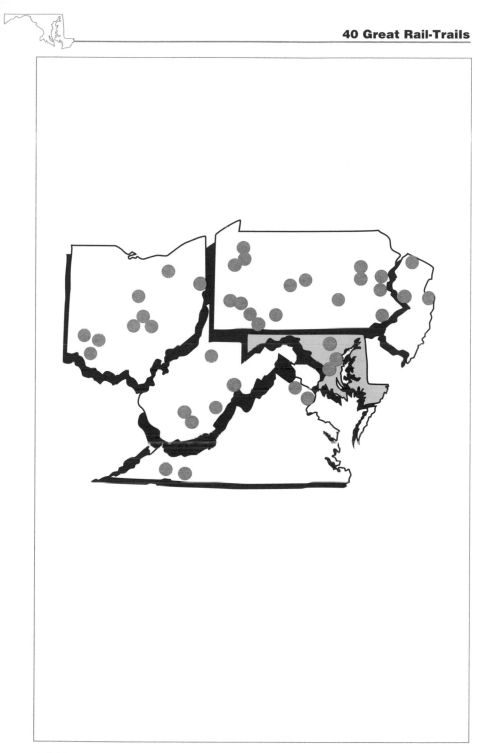

MARYLAND'S GREAT RAIL-TRAILS

1. Baltimore and Annapolis Trail
2. Capital Crescent Trail
3. Northern Central Railroad Trail

Karen-Lee Ryan

In-line skating is one of the most popular activities on the suburban Baltimore and Annapolis Trail.

Baltimore and Annapolis Trail

Endpoints: North Shore of the Severn River to Glen Burnie

Location: Anne Arundel County

Length: 13.3 miles

Surface: Asphalt

Uses:

(in designated areas)

Contact: Dave Dionne, Superintendent
Baltimore and Annapolis Trail Park
P.O. Box 1007
Severna Park, MD 21146
410-222-6244

◆◆◆

With 50 percent of all Anne Arundel County residents living within a mile of the Baltimore and Annapolis Trail (B&A), it is no wonder the trail is known as "Anne Arundel's Backyard." It's a place where people go to chat with neighbors, breathe some fresh air and enjoy every conceivable recreational activity. And, this is a trail that connects community resources together. People use the trail to get to shops, libraries, schools and other community sites.

Originally developed as the Annapolis and Baltimore Short Line, this route was once a key transportation line for passengers and freight. The first train left Annapolis in early 1887, carrying passengers through woods and farmland. Within just a few years several new towns had sprung up along the route.

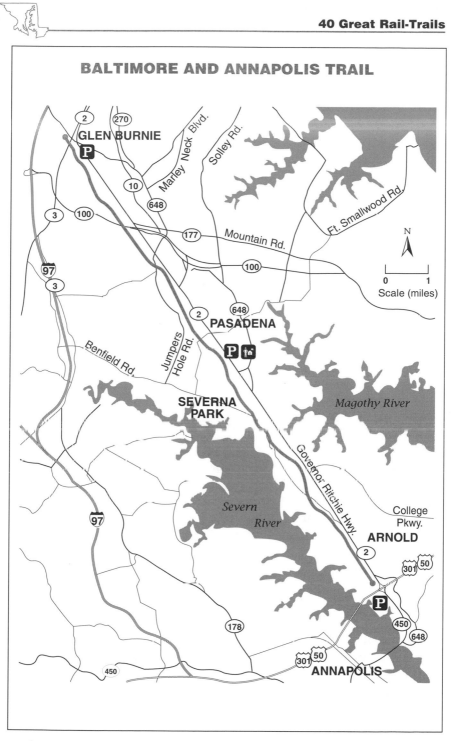

BALTIMORE AND ANNAPOLIS TRAIL

Early on, a reorganization brought a new name—the Baltimore & Annapolis Short Line. Then, in 1906, Maryland Electric Railway took over the operation and electrified the route within two years. Another shift gave the Washington, Baltimore & Annapolis Electric Railroad control of the line in 1921. But, the line went bankrupt, and in 1935, the line was reincorporated as the Baltimore and Annapolis Railroad.

In its peak years, the line carried 1.75 million people between the state capital and Baltimore, with hourly service from 6 a.m. to 11 p.m. Passenger use of the line began to drop in the 1920s and was finally halted in the 1950s. Freight service continued until 1968, when the bridge over the Severn River was condemned.

To get to the trail, take State Route 450 south from U.S. Route 50. Then take the first right into a large parking lot developed for the B & A Trail. Several signs direct you to the start of the trail, which is 0.6 miles from the parking area via a shoulder on Boulters Way.

You will begins the trail in the residential neighborhoods on the northeast side of the Severn River. You will notice immediately that the trail is impeccably maintained, especially considering that more than half a million people use the trail every year. Community groups have adopted sections of the trail, planting and maintaining the flower beds that enhance its appearance.

In less than a mile, you will come to the trail's first picnic tables and shade shelter. Running parallel to the commercially-developed Route 2 (Ritchie Highway), the trail is in close proximity to plenty of restaurants and shops.

At the Jones Station Road crossing (3.4 miles from the start), you will find drinking water, a phone, a shade shelter and benches. Feel free to use the nearby Severna Park "Park 'n Ride" lot. Near the four-mile mark, you'll cross over Round Bay Road before heading into Severna Park. This town once served as a commercial center for farmers and has evolved into a popular suburb of Baltimore.

At the Riggs Avenue crossing, be sure to catch a glimpse of the only brick train station originally built along the line. It doubled as a post office until 1951 and now houses the Severna Park Model Railroad Club. There are a number of shops and restaurants over the next half-mile, all just a block or two from the trail.

At mile marker 7, you will come to another B & A Trail highlight: a Victorian-era train station that has been refurbished and now serves as the ranger station and trail headquarters. Drinking water, picnic tables, bathrooms, a telephone and ample parking are all located here, as well as a wheelchair sports/fitness course.

The next few miles are a mix of old and new homes, as well as some commercial development. The largest structure is the Marley Station Mall, located about 10.5 miles from the start of the trail. An old railroad station once stood at this site, but it was destroyed when the mall was constructed in the mid-1980s. The original railroad grade was also consumed by the mall and its parking lot. The trail weaves around the outskirts of the parking area, with a few hills to make the trip more interesting.

Soon you will cross over Route 100 and then over Marley Creek on a bridge with a colorful history. The original 140-foot railroad

Karen–Lee Ryan

This Victorian-era train station now serves as the trail's ranger station.

bridge was destroyed by Hurricane Agnes in 1972. However, ingenious trail planners located a historic highway bridge in Missouri—available at no cost—and made arrangements to have it taken apart and transported to Maryland and placed on the trail.

In 1989, workers reassembled the bridge, and the county sponsored a dedication to honor its placement onto the trail. Unfortunately, improper lifting of the bridge caused its collapse, and the well-traveled, historic bridge became a pile of scrap as trail enthusiasts watched in disbelief. The construction company then hastily built the bridge that is now on the trail.

Beyond mile marker 11, the trail is sandwiched between rows of houses until it passes by Harundale Mall, the first enclosed mall east of the Mississippi River. A residential area picks up again on the other side of the mall, where there are also a few parking areas for the trail. Most of them are full, even on weekday evenings.

By mile marker 12, you are heading into the city of Glen Burnie, which has gone through extraordinary urban redevelopment in recent years, with the trail in the center of it all. Trail development in this area was funded partially through a Community Development Block Grant. Prior to the trail's construction, the derelict corridor was home to an open-air drug market, and opponents feared the trail would increase vandalism and crime in the area.

One trip through this area proves that nothing could be further from the truth. The well-used and meticulously pruned trail is the pride of the community. A new District Court, as well as a parking garage and movie theaters, are adjacent to the trail. All were part of the successful $25 million renewal project that now serves as a model for other communities.

The Baltimore and Annapolis Trail actually ends at Dorsey Road. Ironically, a new light rail service continues on the corridor—just across Dorsey Road—into Baltimore, as area passenger train service is once again in demand.

Coalition for the Capital Crescent Trail

The Capital Crescent Trail parallels the C&O Canal, a popular
canoeing spot, for nearly four miles.

Capital Crescent Trail

Endpoints: Bethesda to Georgetown

Location: Montgomery County and Washington, D.C.

Length: 7 miles (will be 11 when completed)

Surface: Asphalt

Uses:

Contact: Rich Metzinger, Landscape Architect
National Park Service, National Capital Region
1100 Ohio Drive, S.W.
Washington, D.C. 20242
202-523-5555

Bill Gries, Land Acquisition Specialist
National Capital Park and Planning
Commission
9500 Brunett Avenue
Silver Spring, MD 20901
301-495-2535

f it's true that good things come to those who wait, then the dedicated volunteers who worked to create the Capital Crescent Trail should be rewarded with something truly magnificent. And all early signs indicate that the Capital Crescent Trail will be just that—magnificent.

This C-shaped trail, part of which runs through the heart of Washington, D.C., connects numerous community facilities, including libraries, schools, and shopping centers. The trail also provides easy access to hundreds of businesses and offices located in the nation's capital. In addition, the trail will ultimately join together a

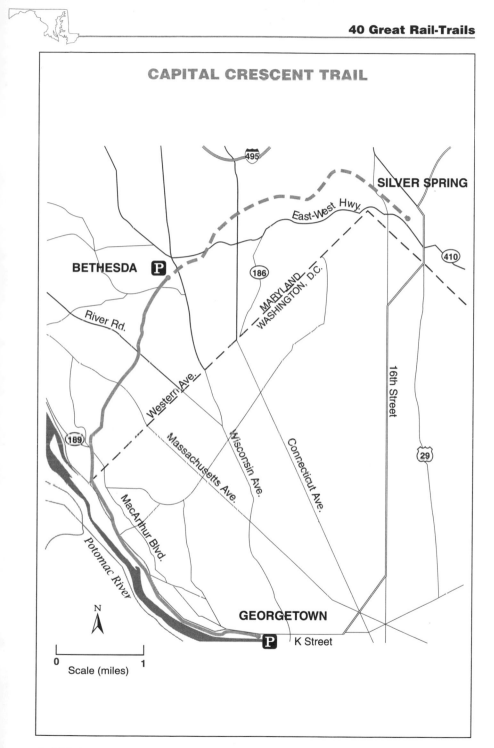

CAPITAL CRESCENT TRAIL

SILVER SPRING

East-West Hwy.

BETHESDA 🅿

River Rd.

Western Ave.

Massachusetts Ave.

Wisconsin Ave.

Connecticut Ave.

16th Street

MacArthur Blvd.

Potomac River

MARYLAND, D.C.
WASHINGTON, D.C.

GEORGETOWN

🅿 K Street

N

0   1
Scale (miles)

dozen parks, including Rock Creek National Park—one of the nation's most heavily used urban parks—and the C&O Canal National Historical Park. The Capital Crescent will also provide the missing link that will connect the metropolitan area's four major multi-use trails.

Sure to attract hundreds of thousands of commuters and recreationists, the Capital Crescent Trail will likely become the national model for urban trails.

Constructed just after the turn of the century, the railroad line was originally known as the Georgetown Branch of the Baltimore and Ohio Railroad. Over the years it hauled coal, fuel, lumber and other building supplies to Washington, D.C., and its close-in suburbs. In recent years, the CSX Corporation had taken over the route, which lost its last customer in 1985. The Coalition for the Capital Crescent Trail soon formed, and advocated a much needed greenway for the rapidly developing metropolitan area.

Because the corridor straddles Montgomery County and the District of Columbia (where it abuts National Park Service property), there was no single entity to take ownership of the line. The

Coalition for the Capital Crescent Trail

In-line skaters try out the newly-paved Capital Crescent Trail.

difficulty of the ownership issue was compounded by the fact that the railroad initially placed the value of the 11-mile corridor at more than $65 million because of the surrounding land values. Eventually the National Park Service purchased the four-mile segment in Washington, and Montgomery County purchased the remaining seven miles in its jurisdiction.

In 1993, after planning was completed and construction funding secured, the first trail sections finally opened. But the Capital Crescent Trail is still a work in progress; while the first seven miles are paved, bridge construction will continue throughout 1995 to make those first seven miles continuous. Amenities will also be developed along the route.

One of the most convenient places to get on the trail is at its current northern terminus in downtown Bethesda. To get there, take Wisconsin Avenue (State Route 355) south from Interstate 495, the Capital Beltway. Travel more than a mile, past the National Institutes of Health buildings, and turn west onto Woodmont Avenue. Proceed about 1.5 miles to the trail, located at the intersection of Bethesda and Woodmont Avenues. A large municipal parking lot is located adjacent to the trail.

The former rail line continues northeast through Bethesda into Silver Spring. The county is investigating the possibility of developing a light rail transit line next to a trail on this section of track. Meanwhile, the trail extension has been stalled. The developed portion of trail travels southwest toward the District. The nearby streets of Bethesda are packed with restaurants, cafes and shops to meet just about any need.

As you head down the trail, you may be surprised by how green and quiet the corridor is, in spite of the urban character of downtown Bethesda. Almost immediately, you will cross over Bradley Boulevard on an old railroad trestle before continuing on behind some apartment buildings.

Within a half-mile, you will reach the Bethesda Pool, one of the many community resources along the Capital Crescent. In the summer, this popular pool teems with people of all ages. Next you will cross over busy Little Falls Parkway at-grade. A median divides the four lanes of traffic, making the crossing more manageable. Soon the trail will bisect the northern portion of Little Falls Park, which continues to line your left side for some distance. Amid the

Coalition for the Capital Crescent Trail

Wildflowers flourish along this urban greenway.

serenity of the trees, wildflowers and birds, you may forget that you are actually cutting through a densely populated area.

After passing behind some residences, you will soon approach River Road, where some commercial developments line the trail. An overpass is slated for development in 1995 to help trail users avoid the heavy traffic on River Road. In the meantime, you may want to cross the road at the Little Falls Road stoplight two blocks south. In another half-mile, you will cross over Massachusetts Avenue on an original stone bridge.

For the next mile, Little Falls Park again lines the trail's left side, providing a peaceful, green environment. After passing the Defense Mapping Agency and viewing the Dalecarlia Reservoir—which provides much of the drinking water for the D.C. area—you will arrive at one of the trail's most stunning features: a 300-foot long, brick-lined tunnel. Passing under MacArthur Boulevard, this tunnel is a hidden treasure many native Washingtonians have never seen.

Soon the trail crosses into the District of Columbia and over the trail's other breathtaking feature: a 300-foot steel railroad trestle

over Arizona Avenue and the C&O Canal. Unfortunately, the bridge has not been re-decked for trail use, so a detour is necessary until the bridge opens in late 1995.

If you have gone as far as the tunnel, you will need to backtrack slightly to where the paved Little Falls Trail passes under the Capital Crescent Trail. Take the Little Falls Trail uphill to MacArthur Boulevard and cross MacArthur to reach Maryland Avenue. Turn left and proceed to Ridge Drive, where you will find a spiral ramp that leads down to Lock 5 on the C&O Canal. Cross over the lock and head south (left) on the canal towpath. Follow the towpath for nearly 1.5 miles and you will arrive back at the Arizona Avenue Bridge. The Capital Crescent Trail resumes paralleling the canal for the remainder of its length.

As you continue south on the Capital Crescent, the canal will be on your left and dense woods will be on your right. If you were to head the other direction on the canal towpath (north), you could go all the way to Cumberland, Maryland, 185 miles from Washington, D.C. You could easily spend days exploring all the C&O National Historical Park's intriguing features along the way.

As you head south, you will pass by Fletcher's Boat House in less than a half-mile, where you can rent canoes. At this point, views of the Potomac River suddenly open up on your right. The river, which separates Washington from Virginia, is wide and scenic. Throughout the year, you may see members of the Georgetown University Crew team sculling along the river. After about 1.5 miles, the Three Sisters Islands rise out of the Potomac River, adding yet another feature to the stunning scenery.

At this point, you are less than a mile from the trail's current endpoint at K Street in Georgetown. Before you get there, you will see the Rosslyn skyline and the multi-arched Key Bridge. You will also pass the Washington Canoe Club and another boat house that offers canoe rentals. From the K Street terminus, where parking is available, the heart of Georgetown is only three blocks north. A popular tourist attraction, this Washington neighborhood is packed with restaurants, cafes, nightclubs and gift shops, many located in attractive and colorful townhouses.

The Capital Crescent Trail will eventually extend nearly another mile parallel to K Street, past the Washington Harbor shops and restaurants, before ending at Rock Creek Parkway and Virginia Avenue.

Northern Central Railroad Trail

Endpoints: Ashland to the Pennsylvania Border

Location: Baltimore County

Length: 20 miles

Surface: Hard-packed crushed limestone

Uses:

Contact: Ms. Peyton Taylor, Area Manager
Gunpowder Falls State Park
P.O. Box 5032
Glen Arm, MD 21057
410-592-2897

◆ ◆ ◆

Since its opening in 1984, the Northern Central Railroad Trail's popularity has grown exponentially. With at least a 50 percent increase in use every year, the Northern Central has quickly become one of the most popular trails in the eastern United States.

This is a corridor packed with history. Opened in 1838, the Northern Central Railroad was one of the nation's earliest rail lines. It crossed the Mason-Dixon line, connecting Baltimore to York, Gettysburg, and Harrisburg, Pennsylvania. During its 138 years of service it carried dairy and other farm products, coal, U.S. mail and Civil War soldiers. But perhaps its biggest claim to fame is that in 1863 it transported President Lincoln to Gettysburg, where he gave his famous address. Ironically, the Northern Central Railroad was one of the lines used to transport the President's body back to Illinois after his assassination.

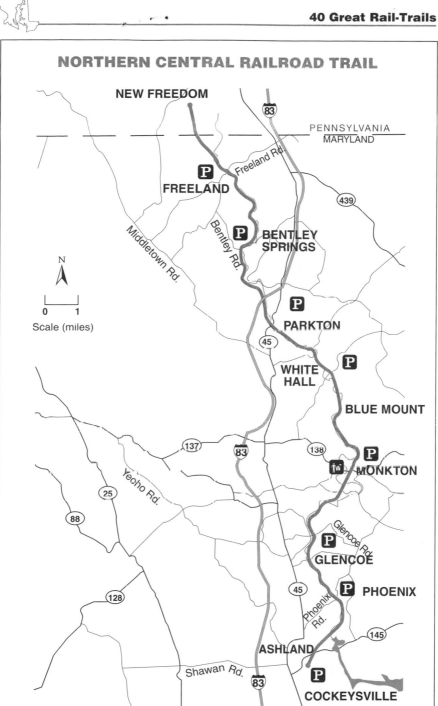

NORTHERN CENTRAL RAILROAD TRAIL

NEW FREEDOM

83

PENNSYLVANIA
MARYLAND

Freeland Rd.

P
FREELAND

439

Middletown Rd.

Bentley Rd.

N

P
BENTLEY
SPRINGS

0   1
Scale (miles)

P
PARKTON

45

WHITE
HALL

P

BLUE MOUNT

137   83   138   **P**
MONKTON

Yeoho Rd.

25

88

Glencoe Rd.

P
GLENCOE

128   45   **P** PHOENIX

Phoenix
Rd.

145

ASHLAND

Shawan Rd.   83

P

COCKEYSVILLE

After more than 120 years in operation, demand for the Northern Central waned. Local passenger service ended in 1959 as cars replaced trains for personal travel. Then in 1972, Hurricane Agnes destroyed bridges on the line, severing all freight and passenger service. In 1976, Penn Central (the route's owner at that time) sold the section closest to Baltimore to the State of Maryland for freight use. Baltimore County convinced the State to apply for a federal rails-to-trails demonstration project grant to fund a portion of trail development for the northern 20 miles.

Because of fierce local opposition, the county decided to drop the rails-to-trails idea. But, the state received a $450,000 federal grant and decided to pick up cautiously where the county had left off. The abandoned corridor had become an eyesore over the years—used primarily as a dumping ground—and adjacent landowners thought a trail would increase the problem.

Just the opposite occurred. Working with hundreds of volunteers, the state cleaned up the route, removing more than 600 tons of trash. Slowly, the old railroad line transformed into a beautiful public park. Although it took nearly 13 years to complete, it was time well spent.

The trail begins in the commercially-developed Hunt Valley area about 15 miles north of Baltimore. To get to the trail's southern

Karen-Lee Ryan

The restored Monkton railroad station sits at the trail's mid-point.

endpoint, take the Shawan Road East exit from Interstate 83; proceed about one mile to Route 45 (York Road) south; go 0.2 miles and turn east onto Ashland Road. Within a half-mile, Ashland Road turns sharply to the right into a new residential development and dead ends at the trail parking lot.

The trail is typically crowded near Ashland, and the parking lot is often full. The recently-built residential development lining the west side of the trail is a reminder of the rapid population growth in northern Baltimore County. Within the first half-mile, you will cross Paper Mill Road at-grade. It is one of the trail's busiest intersections, so use caution.

Soon after that crossing, the trail quickly feels pleasantly remote. Before you reach the first mile marker, you may see a semi-circular stone structure that was formerly a lime kiln. This is the first of many railroad remnants along the Northern Central. Keep your eyes open for some of the smaller artifacts, including switch boxes and whistleposts (small signs with a large "W" that reminded the train engineer to sound his whistle).

On the other side of mile marker 1, you will make your first crossing over the scenic Gunpowder Falls. At Phoenix, near mile marker two, there are a few additional parking spaces, as well as a telephone and portable toilets. A "boat launch" also has been developed here, although it is primarily used by people with canoes and inner tubes.

The 2.5-mile section between Sparks and Corbett Roads are quite striking with woods lining the trail on one side and Gunpowder Falls weaving its way along the other. Many benches and picnic tables have been placed in key locations, so you can take a break and enjoy the scenery. The widest view of Gunpowder Falls is just south of mile marker 6. Soon thereafter, the stream veers away from the trail, but the views open up onto nearby farms before you arrive at the country village of Corbett. From there, proceed to Monkton Station, a Northern Central landmark.

Monkton Station is the heart of the trail, typically bustling with people eager to view the preserved structure that unites the corridor's heritage with its current users. Owned by the Maryland Department of Natural Resources, the station now contains a park office, a railroad museum and a meeting room. During the 1980s, the state led an extensive restoration effort that returned the building to its heyday-era appearance. Today, such modern amenities

G. Frederick Stork

Drifting along the Gunpowder Falls offers an alternate way to see the attractive countryside surrounding the Northern Central.

The hard-packed crushed stone surface of the Northern Central Railroad Trail is suitable for all bicycles.

Maryland Department of Natural Resources

as bathrooms, drinking water and soda machines, meet the needs of trail users.

A few other refreshments are available across the parking lot at a shop that also rents bicycles, inner tubes and canoes. Parking at Monkton Station is quite limited and fills up quickly on weekends.

The five-mile stretch from Monkton to Parkton is wonderfully scenic, as the route is shaped by waterfalls and creeks. North of Monkton, you continue paralleling Gunpowder Falls until you near mile marker 10, where Little Falls lines the corridor and several creeks approach the trail from the east. You will pass through the historic village of White Hall just before mile 11. This former paper mill town offers bathrooms, a telephone, drinking water and parking.

Steep rocky outcroppings line this section of trail, as the scenery seems to keep getting better! You may also find a few swimming holes in this area before reaching Parkton. You can't miss the actual falls of Little Falls as they swirl rapidly through a man-made cut before dropping into a large pool. Stop here to take some pictures or enjoy a picnic lunch overlooking what are actually the trail's biggest falls.

As with most towns along the Northern Central, Parkton (once a railroad hub) offers no amenities except parking and a telephone. North of mile marker 13, you can take advantage of an 18-station exercise course before crossing under Interstate 83. Soon thereafter, the vegetation becomes so thick around the trail that it seems almost tropical for about a mile. On a summer day, this area offers a brief respite from the hot sun and humidity. By mile marker 15, creeks line both sides of the trail. Not surprisingly, this area is a popular spot for fishing, and serves as home for many beavers.

Just north of Bentley Springs, which was once a resort town known for its therapeutic waters, you will find a telephone, a portable toilet, as well about 20 parking spaces. The surrounding topography is primarily rolling hills with lush vegetation. Continuing north toward Freeland, you get some nice vistas of the surrounding farmland, coupled with the rippling flow of Beetree Run. Occasional wetlands also line the corridor. Along the trail in Freeland are restrooms, a telephone, picnic tables and a good-sized parking lot.

Once you pass the parking area in Freeland, you are 1.3 miles from the Pennsylvania border, where the York County Heritage Trail continues on the same corridor. If you have the energy, travel the short distance to New Freedom, Pennsylvania, where you'll find an old train station, a couple of restaurants and a bike shop, as well as a preserved caboose and three railroad passenger cars.

Once you cross the state line, the trail takes on a slightly different feel. A tunnel of trees envelops the trail, which has been developed next to an inactive set of tracks. The surface is not as hard-packed as the Northern Central, but that may change as it gets more use.

Currently the York County Heritage Trail is only 1.5 miles, but eventually it will continue another 18.5 miles to downtown York—creating a 40-mile continuous trail corridor. This extension will undoubtedly draw even more users to the already popular Northern Central Trail.

An Introduction to Rail-Trails in Virginia

Virginia is for lovers—lovers of long rail-trails through breathtaking scenery. While the state has only nine rail-trails totaling 160 miles, it boasts three rail-trails longer than 30 miles that cut through Virginia's famed countryside.

In the early 20th century, thousands of miles of railroads cut across Virginia, transporting freight—such as timber, iron ore and lead—as well as passengers. As with the other states in the Mid-Atlantic, other forms of transportation have caused serious decline in the railroad industry. Fortunately, a number of railroad corridors have been saved and are now serving hikers, bicyclists, equestrians and other trail users.

While no statewide rails-to-trails organization exists, most rail-trails and trail projects have an active citizen support group. And the agencies managing rail-trails throughout the state range from municipality to county and from regional to federal. The existing, high-quality trails serve as models for the 18 new trail projects underway.

The four trails selected for this book highlight the striking beauty of Virginia. From suburban Washington, D.C., to remote southwestern Virginia, these trails are sure to please.

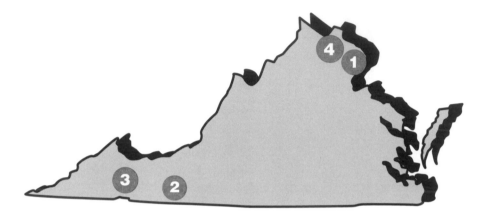

VIRGINIA'S GREAT RAIL-TRAILS

1. Accotink Trail
2. New River Trail State Park
3. Virginia Creeper National Recreational Trail
4. Washington & Old Dominion Railroad Regional Park

Karen-Lee Ryan

Many people enjoy strolling under the Accotink Trail's canopy of trees.

Accotink Trail

Endpoints: Springfield

Location: Fairfax County

Length: 2.2 miles of a 3.75-mile trail is on an abandoned rail line

Surface: gravel and dirt

Uses: 🚶 🚲 🏇 🎣 ⛷

Contact: Kurt Kincannon
Park Specialist II
Lake Accotink Park
Fairfax County Park Authority
3701 Pender Drive
Fairfax, VA 22030
703-569-0285

◆ ◆ ◆

L ess than 20 miles from the heart of Washington, D.C. lies a park where time seems to have stood still. As soon as you enter Lake Accotink Park, you will notice an old-fashioned carousel, a lake teeming with paddle boats and a trestle overhead where an occasional train chugs by.

In what feels like a 1950s family day-trip destination, you can rent a canoe, play miniature golf, initiate a volleyball game, go fishing, grill some burgers or just enjoy a picnic under the shade trees. You can also take a walk on the rail-trail. Or, if you prefer mountain biking, you can venture off onto nearly 18 miles of adjacent mountain bicycling trails.

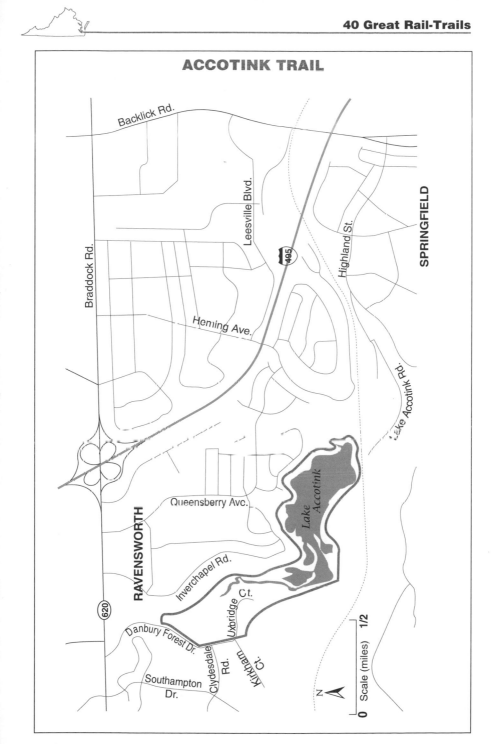

ACCOTINK TRAIL

Backlick Rd.

Leesville Blvd.

Braddock Rd.

Heming Ave.

495

Highland St.

SPRINGFIELD

Lake Accotink Rd.

Lake Accotink

Queensberry Ave.

RAVENSWORTH

Inverchapel Rd.

Uxbridge Ct.

620

Danbury Forest Dr.

Clydesdale Rd.

Kirkham Ct.

Southampton Dr.

N

Scale (miles)

0   1/2

A portion of the Accotink Trail began in 1850 as a segment of the Orange and Alexandria Railroad. Originally transporting goods from the port of Alexandria to the farms in Manassas, the line played an important role during the Civil War, providing supplies to Union and Confederate troops. During Reconstruction, the line merged with the Manassas Gap Railroad, which went bankrupt in 1871.

To get to Lake Accotink Park, take Braddock Road east (exit 5) from the Capital Beltway (Interstate 495). In less than two miles, you will take Backlick Road south to Highland Street, where you will turn right; take another right onto Lake Accotink Road and turn left into the park.

Half of the four-mile trail that encircles Lake Accotink is on an abandoned rail corridor. It begins below the tall trestle, and after a short uphill scramble, the trail quickly becomes wooded and fairly curvy. When the peaceful trail straightens out and gets wider, you will know you are on the former rail corridor. Keep your eyes out for a remnant railroad spike left over from a bygone era.

Wetlands sporadically line either side of the trail, where you might see a few interesting birds and other wildlife. Within about

Karen-Lee Ryan

The Accotink Trail offers great views to the popular Accotink Lake.

1.5 miles, the Accotink Trail branches off to the right. The rail-trail continues straight ahead for another 1.5 miles, with the last half-mile doubling as a service road for a power sub-station. The rail-trail ends abruptly at Rolling Road.

To continue encircling the lake on the Accotink Trail, take the marked turnoff to the right. It leads you directly to Danbury Forest Drive. You will pass a public pool on the left and an elementary school on the right. After crossing Lonsdale Drive, the trail resumes off to the right and quickly crosses over Accotink Creek. From here, it is less than 2 miles from the parking lot where you started the trail.

This section of trail is fairly wooded, and it also passes by many local residences. As you get closer to the marina and back toward your starting point, you can take a couple of short side paths off to the right toward the water's edge. From there, you will get some great views of the lake and the railroad trestle.

If you have time after you complete the trail, rent a canoe, play some volleyball or enjoy a ride on the carousel.

New River Trail State Park

Endpoints: Pulaski to Galax with a spur to Fries

Location: Grayson, Wythe, Carroll and Pulaski Counties

Length: 55 miles (will be 57 miles when completed)

Surface: Dirt and gravel and cinders

Uses:

Contact: Mark Hufeisen
New River Trail State Park
Route 1, Box 81X
Austinville, VA 24312
703-699-6778*

◆◆◆

The New River Trail State Park has some interesting ironies. For much of its length, the 57-mile trail parallels the New River, which is actually one of the world's oldest river. And, while the New River Trail is one of Virginia's newest state parks, the history of the route dates back thousands of years.

Tucked in the lush Appalachian Mountains of southwestern Virginia, the path now occupied by Virginia's only state managed rail-trail got its start as a Native American footpath. Centuries later, German, Scottish, Irish and English immigrants settled this area that was rich in minerals.

In the early 1880s, the Norfolk and Western Railway Company began building its Cripple Creek Branch to transport the plentiful

---

* The area code for southwestern Virginia changes to 540 in July 1995

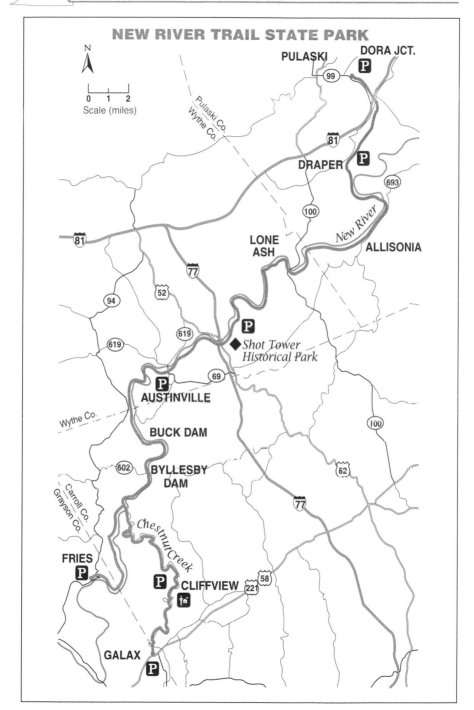

NEW RIVER TRAIL STATE PARK

N

0   1   2
Scale (miles)

PULASKI

DORA JCT.

99

Pulaski Co.
Wythe Co.

81

DRAPER

693

100

New River

LONE
ASH

ALLISONIA

81

77

52

94

619

619

Shot Tower
Historical Park

69

AUSTINVILLE

Wythe Co.

BUCK DAM

100

602

BYLLESBY
DAM

52

77

Carroll Co.
Grayson Co.

Chestnut Creek

FRIES

CLIFFVIEW

58

221

GALAX

Karen-Lee Ryan

The Fries Branch of the New River Trail offers great views of the area's rural landscapes.

iron and lead that were being mined in the area. Over the years, the line also hauled timber, livestock, furniture and passengers. The last train ran on the tracks in October, 1985, and a few months later, Norfolk Southern donated the line to the state for development as a linear park.

Virginia's first state park rail-trail has been under development ever since, increasing the tourism potential for the rural towns the trains once served. The trail is a work in progress, and unfortunately, its two unopened miles are smack in the middle of the trail. The State is trying to acquire those two miles, which have been declared private property. For trail users, the only alternate route is a cumbersome (and hilly) series of developed and undeveloped roads.

With this in mind, you might opt to tour this trail in two separate segments. The enterprising owner of a bike shop located adjacent to the trail in Draper (just south of Pulaski) recently established a shuttle service that enables trail users to travel the trail in one direction. For more information call New River Bicycles at 703-980-1741.*

Galax to Shot Tower Historic Park and the Branch to Fries

The southernmost end of the trail begins in Galax, about five miles west of Interstate 77 on U.S. Routes 58/221. A parking area is located on the right side of the road just before you enter downtown Galax. A larger parking area with horse trailer parking is located in Cliffview, about two miles northeast of Galax. An information office, restrooms and a convenience store are also located here. These comprise the majority of the trail's amenities, so make good use of them.

Beginning in Galax, the trail parallels the scenic Chestnut Creek and travels through rolling hills and farmland. The trail offers a remote peacefulness with great scenery and the soothing sound of the creek flowing nearby. You'll also find a few signs of the industry that once dotted the area. Beyond the original mile marker "P 47," which indicates that you are 47 miles from Pulaski, you may see the site once occupied by the General Chemical Company.

The trail surface is fairly rugged in this section and continues for several miles with large, chunky gravel. But, the pristine views, numerous river crossings and abundant wildlife should keep you energized. By mile marker 42 (the numbers go down as you get closer to Pulaski), the surface becomes smoother. Steep, rocky outcroppings begin to envelop the trail's left side and the trail corridor hugs the creek.

After mile marker 41, you will come to one of the trail's unique features: a curved tunnel with significantly different openings on either end. Take a moment to look at the design of each opening as you enter and exit the tunnel. Because of its curvature, the tunnel will look pitch black before you enter it, although once you are just inside, you will see light coming from the other end.

Within less than a mile, you will reach the trail's longest bridge span at Fries Junction. This 1,089 foot curved bridge span is where the trail actually meets up with the New River, which has an uncommon south to north flow.

The five-mile Fries (pronounced "freeze") Branch of the New River Trail goes off to the left at the end of this bridge, paralleling the New River for its entire length. This section of the trail offers some of the best views of the New River, which is quite wide along this section of trail. The spur "ends" in Fries although the town's

Near Fries Junction on the New River Trail State Park.

motto is, "the trail starts here." You will pass by a convenience store before reaching Fries, which seems to be struggling from the loss of industry in the area.

The main trail leads to the right at the end of the long bridge span, past a couple of picnic tables and a shade shelter. A large picnic area is off to the trail's left side just before you cross over the next bridge span. On the other side of the bridge, if you look to the left, you will see a wooden shelter that surrounds a portable toilet.

For the next several miles the river views are quite striking. Near mile marker 37, you will pass by Byllesby Dam, and three miles later, you will reach Buck Dam. The stretch in between is somewhat overgrown, with a few patches of thick gravel, but it is still easily passable. Primitive camping is possible on National Forest Service property in this area.

Prior to mile marker 30, you will cross over the Ivanhoe Bridge, the trail's third longest at 670 feet. In 1917, Ivanhoe was home to the nation's first carbide plant and was surrounded by a number of iron furnaces and lead mines. The extensive remains of the abandoned Austinville Lead Mines parallel the trail beginning beyond

◆ 163 ◆

mile marker 30. Closed in 1981, the mines had been in operation since 1756, providing most of the lead for the Revolutionary War and for the Confederacy in the Civil War.

About a half-mile beyond the industrial site, you will come to the trail's second tunnel, which is shorter and straight. Beyond the tunnel, the trail is in great shape. And, the surface is noticeably smoother as you near the Shot Tower Historical Park and the trail's midpoint. This area is one of the trail's prettiest sections, with some steep rock outcroppings on one side and good views of the expansive river on the other.

You will pass under Interstate 77 just prior to arriving at Shot Tower Historical Park. You can get to the tower, which is only open on weekends, via a loop trail that includes a number of steps; signs are posted on the trail. Built in the early 1800s, Shot Tower ascends 75 feet, which is half the distance thought necessary to shape falling molten metal into shot for Civil War weapons. A lower shaft once dropped another 75 feet from the tower floor to the river level, where the shot was cooled before being transported to troops.

The park offers ample trail parking, as well as restrooms and picnic tables. The trail headquarters are located near the entrance

The New River Trail's picturesque Hiwassee Trestle.

Karen-Lee Ryan

to the parking lot. This section of trail "ends" just beyond the tower, where a sign indicates, "Trail Ends 300 Feet." For details on how to get around the detour, it is best to talk with the park staff, but keep in mind that the office is closed on the weekends.

East of Shot Tower to Pulaski

On the east side of the "detour" heading toward Pulaski, the river continues to parallel the trail on its north side as steep walls of rock line the trail's south side. The combination of these features, coupled with the sounds of rippling water and singing cicadas during the summer, make this section of trail particularly captivating.

The first point of interest is located at the somewhat obscured 22.7 mile marker. If you look carefully, you will find several old wooden steps that lead to an intriguing stone arch, which houses an old spring house under the trail. It once served as a refrigerator for a nearby farmer. In less than three miles, you will arrive at what remains of Bertha, the former site of the Bertha Lead and Zinc Company.

The next few miles are shrouded by trees, a refreshing respite on a hot summer day. At mile marker 17.4 a cryptic sign reads "Warning Unsafe Structure—Keep Off," although no structure is visible. The sign refers to the former Barren Springs furnace, which looks like a large rock formation concealed by vegetation. After passing under State Route 100, the views of the river really begin to open up on the left side and the walls of rock get steeper on the right.

As you cross into Pulaski County, indicated by a stone marker, you will see the trail's first small rest area. Near mile marker 14, you'll pass the remnants of a former ore washer and in less than a mile you will cross over a bridge about one mile west of Allisonia. This town once served as headquarters for five mining operations. There are no trail-related services here, although parking is available.

One of the trail's most stunning features is the 951-foot Hiwassee Bridge. Built in 1831, the bridge now offers trail users excellent views of the New River. Within a mile, the trail begins an uphill climb to Draper, and by mile marker 8, you will cross over

the trail's highest bridge, the Delton Trestle, as the trail veers away from the New River.

Beyond this point, the views change to rolling farmland as you ease into the town of Draper. Portable toilets and parking are located here.

At mile marker 5, the trail begins its descent into Pulaski. At marker 2.6, you will see the only original railroad crossing signal that remains on the entire 57 mile route—it now signals your final approach into Pulaski. The trail currently ends at a trailhead in Dora Junction, about a mile shy of downtown Pulaski.

If you prefer, you can begin your journey at this end of the trail. To reach this trailhead, take the Route 99 exit from Intestate 81. Following the New River Trail signs, go north two miles and turn right on Xaloy Drive to the parking area.

Virginia Creeper
National Recreation Trail

Endpoints: White Top to Abingdon

Location: Washington and Grayson Counties

Length: 34 miles

Surface: Dirt and gravel

Uses:

Contact: *White Top–Damascus Section*
Area Ranger
Mt. Rogers National Recreation Area
Route 1, Box 303
Marion, VA 24354
703-783-5196*

Damascus–Abingdon Section
Abingdon Convention and Visitors Bureau
335 Cummings Street
Abingdon, VA 24210
800-435-3440

◆◆◆

I f you think all rail-trails are flat or have only a gentle grade, riding on this trail will change your mind in a hurry. With a 1,500 foot drop in elevation and grades of up to six percent, this trail will literally move you. At the same time its breathtaking

* The area code for southwestern Virginia changes to 540 in July 1995

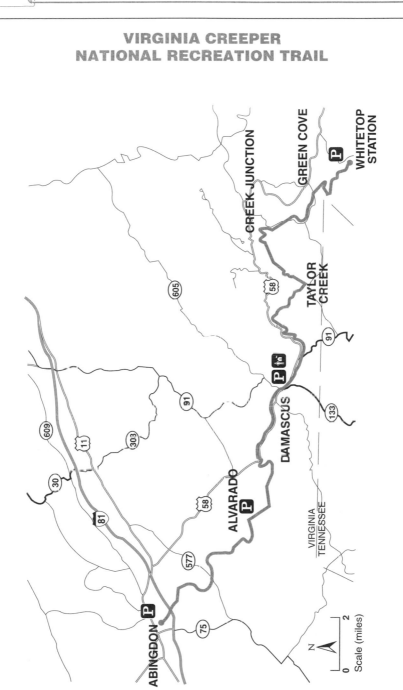

VIRGINIA CREEPER
NATIONAL RECREATION TRAIL

mountain views, rippling creeks and nearly 100 bridges and trestles will transport you to a new dimension.

Of course, it's easiest to start at the top, and the entrepreneurial founder of the local Blue Blaze Shuttle Service has made that easy for you. The shuttle will bring you and your bike from Damascus or Abingdon to the peak of the Virginia Creeper Trail. Then, you return to your car at your own pace. On the other hand, you can always start at the bottom and work your way up to the top. For more information, call Blue Blaze Shuttle Service at 703-475-5095.*

Taking its name from the early locomotives that struggled up the corridor's steep grades, the Virginia Creeper Trail actually got its start thousands of years ago as a Native American footpath. Centuries later, Daniel Boone and other European pioneers explored the foot trail.

At the start of the 20th Century, the Virginia-Carolina Railroad was constructed to haul lumber, iron ore and passengers. It was one of the steepest standard-gauge railroads in the East. The last train ran on the line in March 1977, and now the route has come full circle as hikers, mountain bicyclists and equestrians enjoy the remote serenity of this rail-trail.

To get to the trail's highest point at Whitetop Station, take U.S. Route 58 east more than 20 miles from Interstate 81; take a right onto Route 726 and follow signs to Whitetop Station. Trailside parking is available one mile past Whitetop. Starting from this point, the trail continues southeast one mile to the North Carolina border, where the corridor once continued for another 45 miles. Unfortunately, the state and local municipalities did not act to preserve the corridor and much of the land reverted to adjacent landowners.

North Carolina residents, however, have witnessed the economic impact of the Virginia Creeper Trail and are now trying to piece together a trail of their own. If you travel the short stretch to the border, the trail becomes noticeably more rugged—and eventually impassable—the further south you go. And remember, you need to go back uphill to get back to Whitetop Station.

Today, Whitetop (elevation 3,576) barely makes it onto most maps, yet in 1915 it was a booming town of 6,000 people, virtually all supporting the logging industry. In fact, at one point, Washington County exported more timber than any other area in the nation.

The three miles from Whitetop to Green Cove feature the trail's steepest downhill sections. Be cautious; it is easy to exceed speeds of 20 miles-per-hour on a bike, and the trail surface is occasionally washed out or excessively gravely.

The mountain views open up quite a bit near mile marker "A 31," an original railroad marker that still accurately marks the distance of 31 miles from Abingdon. You will enter Green Cove before you reach mile marker 30. After a road crossing, bear slightly to the left to stay on the trail, and you will see the Green Cove train station. It is the only one still standing along the entire route. Open on Fridays, Saturdays and Sundays during summer, the station is worth a visit. Over the years it has doubled as a post office and a pharmacy, and memorabilia of each are on view inside the building.

More great views of the surrounding mountains and the parallel creek open up after the station. You will also cross a number of trestles, which require caution as signs and posts are often located at either end. This section's few road crossings have cumbersome gates that can be difficult to maneuver with a bike even at low speeds.

A little more than four miles from Green Cove, you will cross the trail's highest and longest bridge span at Creek Junction. With a length of 550 feet and a height of more than 100 feet, it doesn't matter what direction you look—all the views are great!

The next few miles seem level compared to the initial steep grades, and the vegetation is lush. In mid-summer, thousands of rhododendrons are in full bloom along the rocky cliffs that line the trail. Wildlife is abundant and includes black bear, bobcat and beaver. You can also walk down to the creek from several spots along this section of trail.

About nine miles from Whitetop, mountains rise gradually in the foreground, framing the gorge that encompasses the trail. In this area you'll find several pleasant spots for camping, which is allowed in many sections along the Jefferson National Forest section of the trail. In another 1.5 miles, the trail passes through a tiny hamlet, where entrepreneurs have placed vending machines along the trail. The next town, Taylor Creek, has a few more homes, a picnic area, a portable toilet and a red caboose.

After passing a sign indicating that you are six miles from

One of the Virginia Creeper's two curved, wooden trestles.

Damascus, you begin a gradual descent into the town. The flowing water, dense woodlands, jagged rocks and arresting mountains make this section of trail one of the most memorable.

Just less than two miles from Damascus, the trail begins to parallel Route 58 and crosses a couple of trestles. You'll know you

are entering the town when you see the municipal swimming pool on the left side. For a small fee, you can take a dip.

The Damascus Trailhead is surrounded by an extensive community park, which includes flush toilets, drinking water, picnic tables, grills, plenty of parking, a small playground and a refurbished caboose, which now serves as a trail information office. The Appalachian Trail and the Virginia Creeper are the same trail

Karen-Lee Ryan

The 550-foot bridge at Creek Junction.

through Damascus, which offers a convenience store and other amenities.

Traveling through Damascus, which is about 15 miles from Abingdon, you continue to parallel Route 58 on a fairly rough trail surface. The next couple of miles are a bit untended and overgrown in places. After the trail goes under Route 58, the trail takes on a more serene tone, although the surface remains rugged. Soon, you will come to the first in a series of gates, indicating your entrance onto private property. The gates serve primarily to contain cattle, so be sure to close them. And, don't disturb any of the animals that you are likely to see.

About nine miles outside of Abingdon, you will pass through the town of Alvarado, where parking is available. In another mile or so, you will cross over a an eye-catching wooden trestle that curves above the widening creek. The next couple of miles rival earlier stretches of the trail for spectacular scenery. The views may keep your mind off the fact that you are beginning a steady ascent into Abingdon. When you reach the second curved wooden trestle it will be easy to see how high you've climbed.

Almost immediately after this trestle, you will continue straight on the trail through another gate; do not bear to the left. Again, be sure to close the gate after you've passed through it. Next you will see a mileage marker indicating that you are now only six miles from Abingdon. The next couple of miles offer more trestles as the trail cuts through the picturesque mountains.

When you get within three miles of Abingdon, you will notice mile markers every half-mile. You will know you are getting close to civilization when the trail is sandwiched between a new home development and a golf course, followed soon after by the Interstate 81 overpass.

The trail's final trestle brings you directly into the Abingdon trailhead, which features one of the line's original steam locomotives. Be sure to take a look at it before heading into Abingdon, which is the oldest town west of the Blue Ridge Mountains.

To get into the town of Abingdon from the trailhead, cross over the active railroad tracks and travel two blocks to quaint Main Street. Most of the town's sights, such as the Barter Theatre and the Martha Washington Inn are to the left. The town, which is a Virginia historic landmark, also has plenty of restaurants and shops where you can relax after a full day on the trail.

G. Frederick Stork

The W&OD encourages a wide range of trail users.

Washington and Old Dominion Railroad Regional Park

Endpoints: Arlington to Purcellville

Location: Arlington, Fairfax and Loudon Counties

Length: 45 miles

Surface: Asphalt with a parallel crushed stone path for 32.5 miles

Uses:

 between Vienna and Purcellville

Contact: Paul McCray, Park Manager
Northern Virginia Regional Park Authority
5400 Ox Road
Fairfax Station, VA 22039
703-729-0596

◆◆◆

With more than two million users every year, northern Virginia's Washington and Old Dominion Railroad Regional Park (W&OD) is the most popular rail-trail in America. The trail hosts a variety of recreational activities, and thousands of bicycle commuters use the trail each week. The W&OD also provides direct access to several other trails in the region. The trail is even shared several by several public utilities, ranging from power lines to fiber optic cables.

WASHINGTON AND OLD DOMINION RAILROAD REGIONAL PARK

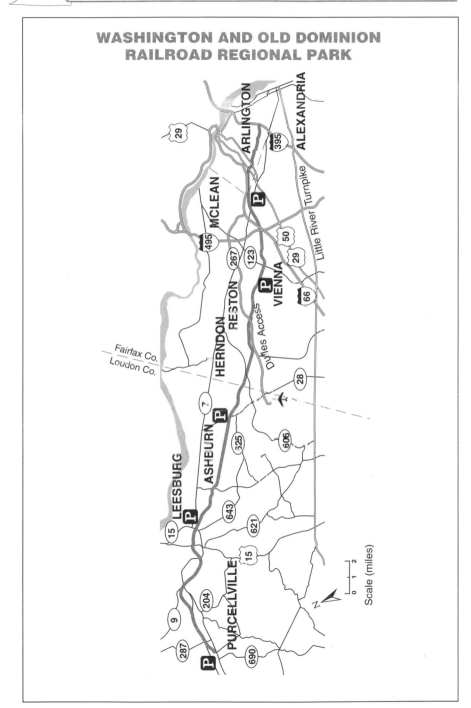

Beginning in 1859, the Washington & Old Dominion Railroad operated on this corridor, although within a decade the line was almost destroyed by the Civil War. Rebuilt after the war, the line reached it peak after the turn of the century, operating both as a passenger and a freight route.

When the trains stopped running in 1968, the Virginia Electric and Power Company purchased the line for its power lines as the suburbs of the nation's capital continued to expand. After 10 years of unsuccessful attempts, the Northern Virginia Regional Park Authority finally won an agreement with VEPCO to purchase the right-of-way over a period of years. The purchase was completed in 1982 and trail development got underway.

Today, the W&OD is the most heavily-used rail-trail in the nation. And while the trail gets its share of tourists, the vast majority of users are from the communities surrounding the trail—many of whom use it daily. Just as the trains helped people escape the rigors of city life by transporting them to the Virginia countryside, the trail today offers people a peaceful setting away from the congested hustle and bustle of the ever-growing suburbia.

The W&OD trail officially begins at Four Mile Run Drive and Shirlington Roads in Arlington, just a couple of blocks from the Village at Shirlington. Heading south from Washington, D.C., take the Shirlington exit from Interstate 395, bear right onto Shirlington Road (north); proceed about a block to South Four Mile Run Drive. The W&OD is easy to spot on this end even from some distance because of the readily-visible high tension power lines. Parking is on-street and limited in this area.

The first section of trail parallels Four Mile Run Drive and includes a number of at-grade crossings. While this area is a mix of commercial and residential apartment buildings, the trail has a surprisingly green feel to it, with the first in a series of community gardens appearing near the trail within the first mile. And, a limited number of parking spaces border the trail just before it crosses Columbia Pike, South Arlington's main thoroughfare.

The next mile or two feel less urban, thanks in part to a stream rippling nearby. As you traverse Arlington County, you will pass through several community parks. A large one, Bluemont Park, may divert you to such recreational amenities as tennis courts, softball fields, volleyball pits and picnic tables. Ample parking is also

available at the park, and many people start the trail here. You may even want to venture two blocks uphill from Bluemont Park on Wilson Boulevard to Upton Hill Regional Park, which features a spectacular 18-hole miniature golf course, a large outdoor swimming pool, a batting cage, drinking water and restrooms.

On the other side of Wilson Boulevard, you will head toward Falls Church. First, you'll skirt the edge of the East Falls Church Metro Station, where the bike racks fill up almost as fast as the parking lot. Just after mile marker 7, you will cross over Route 7— and its numerous shops and fast food chains—on the trail's newest and longest bridge. This crossing, formerly one of the most cumbersome and treacherous on the trail, is now a snap thanks to the new bridge.

Next, you will parallel Shreve Road for a stretch, until the trail crosses over Interstate 66 and passes by Idylwood Park before crossing Interstate 495, the Capital Beltway. Once outside the beltway, the trail cuts through a more residential and wooded area as it weaves its way toward Vienna. Near the 11.5 mile marker and Park Avenue, you will find a community center, restrooms, drinking water and plenty of parking.

Maple Avenue is the next road you will cross, and there are plenty of places to stop for a bite to eat. You may want to have a picnic at Vienna Centennial Park, located a block from Maple, where you will find a restored red caboose, picnic tables and benches in a pleasant setting. Parking is also available.

You may also catch a glimpse of the old Vienna railroad station as you head back toward residential developments after passing by several commercial buildings. At this point, the parallel equestrian trail begins and the trail becomes more scenic despite the power lines overhead. Just before mile marker 13, you'll pass under the first of three stone arch bridges developed along the corridor before the Civil War. The next road crossing is a couple of miles away as you enter the planned community of Reston at Hunter Mill Road.

In another mile, be cautious crossing busy Sunrise Valley Drive at grade. Fortunately, the trail passes under the heavily-traveled Dulles Access Toll Road. The trail continues its sheltered feel for several miles, although you are never far from Reston's many activities, restaurants and shops. There is a large commuter parking

G. Frederick Stork

Many people with disabilities use the W&OD.

lot along the trail at Sunset Hill Road in Reston that can be used for trail parking on weekends.

You will pass the old Reston Train station and some picnic tables. Beyond mile marker 18 on the community's western edge, you will cross Reston Parkway, home to the Reston Town Center shopping and restaurant complex.

The trail's second stone arch bridge is located just beyond mile marker 19, followed by a bridge over Herndon Parkway. Within a mile, you will enter the older area of Herndon, where another caboose and train station have been refurbished amid several restaurants and shops. Next, you'll pass through Bready Park, which has an 18-hole golf course, baseball diamonds, tennis courts, picnic tables and bathrooms. The Herndon Community Center is also nearby.

The continuing suburban sprawl of northern Virginia is quite evident over the next several miles as you pass by numerous new housing developments (and some commercial developments) abutting the trail. Interestingly, many of the builders use the proximity of their properties to the W&OD as a selling point in their advertising.

Just beyond mile marker 24, you will cross over several lanes of Sully Road, where parking is available. Beyond this point, development temporarily subsides and the rolling, green landscape of once-rural Loudon County can be viewed in the distance. After a few more bridges, you will head into Ashburn, a rapidly growing, planned community that has dramatically changed the face of the area in the last few years.

The level of construction begins to diminish outside of Ashburn. Near mile marker 30 you'll cut through an active quarry and cross over Goose Creek on a bridge that has been destroyed and rebuilt several times, although its piers date back to pre-Civil War years. The next several miles of trail are peaceful and more scenic once the high tension lines end at mile marker 31.

Leesburg is the next historic town along the trail, which detours off the original railroad alignment to get under U.S. Route 15 on the edge of town. A community center is located about a mile from here, where you can stop and use the restrooms and refill water bottles.

The western end of the W&OD Trail highlights the disappearing rural landscapes of northern Virginia.

Once in Leesburg, home to much Civil War memorabilia, there are plenty of places to visit. Stop by the Market Station Visitors Center (open seven days a week) to pick up information about what to do in the area. Signs on the trail direct you to the center. King Street is the town's main street and also the site of the old Leesburg train station. After crossing over the Route 7 bypass, the area surrounding the trail is markedly more rural. And, the views of nearby farms offer a glimpse into Loudon County's past.

You will ascend through an area known as Clark's Gap, where the views seem to get prettier all the time. You will cross under the third stone arch bridge just prior to making a steep climb as part of a half-mile detour around Route 7 via Route 9. Once on the other side of the detour, you are six miles from Purcellville, and you are on the trail's shadiest section.

Farmland continues to line the trail as you approach Purcellville. Beyond mile marker 42, you are paralleling the Route 7 Bypass, which usually has little traffic. At this point, you start getting some great vistas of the Blue Ridge Mountains, and your legs may begin to notice that you are already in the foothills.

The trail will make one last diversion off the railroad grade to bypass Route 287. The half-mile detour is fairly obvious and usually signed. Once back on the trail, you will make the one-mile descent into Purcellville, a once-bustling trading center. You will see the not-yet-renovated Purcellville train station just prior to the trail's end, two blocks north of Main Street. You will pass a couple of restaurants and shops on 21st Street en route to Main Street.

An Introduction to Rail-Trails in West Virginia

With a dozen rail-trails totaling nearly 200 miles, West Virginia is a great state for rail-trail enthusiasts—especially for those who like a more rugged experience. Home to several state park rail-trails, including the 75-mile Greenbrier River Trail and the 60-mile North Bend Rail-Trail, West Virginia is a state dedicated to attracting visitors to see this "wild, wonderful" place.

Railroads once criss-crossed the state, serving the coal, petroleum and timber industries. During the 20th century, the railroads have steadily declined as the industries throughout the state waned. But many communities, suffering economically from the loss of industry, are banking on trail-related tourism to ease the slump and preserve some of the state's industrial heritage.

The citizen-based West Virginia Rails-to-Trails Council promotes the state's trails, and various local rail-trail organizations champion individual projects. Recently, a statewide assessment of abandoned rail corridors targeted nearly 30 lines as having priority for rail-trail conversions. When these trails are developed, West Virginia will have a truly magnificent network of trails.

This book will lead you to several existing rail-trails that highlight the steep mountains, deep valleys, rippling rivers and remote towns that clearly illustrate West Virginia's wild and wonderful reputation.

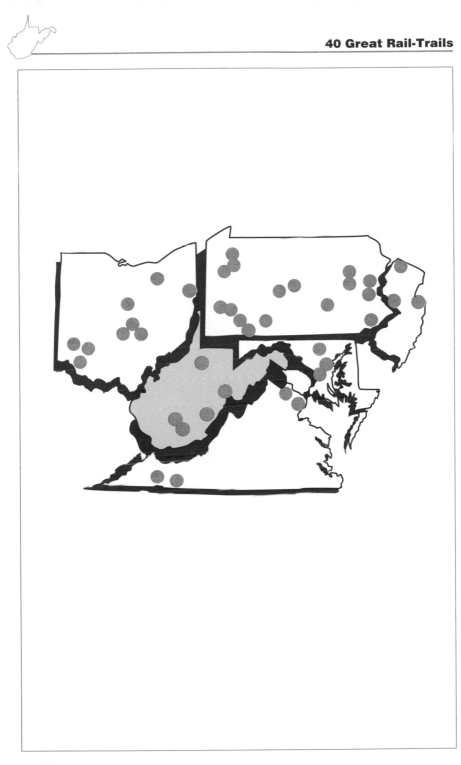

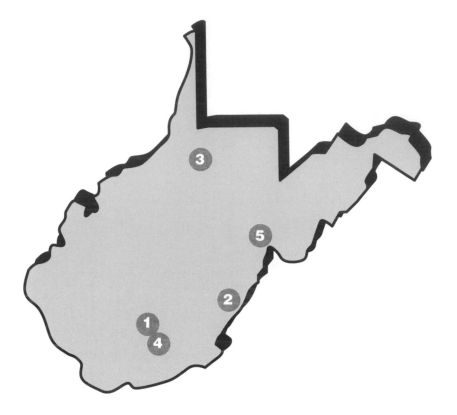

WEST VIRGINIA'S GREAT RAIL-TRAILS

1. Glade Creek Trail
2. Greenbrier River Trail
3. North Bend Rail-Trail
4. Thurmond to Minden Trail
5. West Fork Trail

Karen-Lee Ryan

The rugged Glade Creek Trail offers a remote retreat for hikers and anglers.

Glade Creek Trail

Endpoints: Within the boundaries of the New River Gorge National River area

Location: Raleigh County

Length: 5.6 miles

Surface: Dirt and gravel

Uses:

Contact: Superintendent
National Park Service
New River Gorge National River
P.O. Box 246
Glen Jean, WV 25846
304-465-0508

◆◆◆

Located in one of the most remote areas of the National Park Service's New River Gorge area, this trail embodies quiet isolation. The Glade Creek ripples peacefully alongside the trail and acts as a soothing presence throughout the entire trip.

Traversing an old narrow gauge railroad route, the Glade Creek Trail has slightly steeper grades than many rail-trails. This corridor, originally developed by the Glade Creek Coal and Lumber Company Railway, transported timber from the nearby mountaintops to a mill in the former town of Hamlet.

The trail begins at the bottom of a dirt access road at the confluence of the New River and Glade Creek. You may want to start your trip from the New River Gorge National River headquarters, located just off U.S. Route 19 in Glen Jean eight miles north of

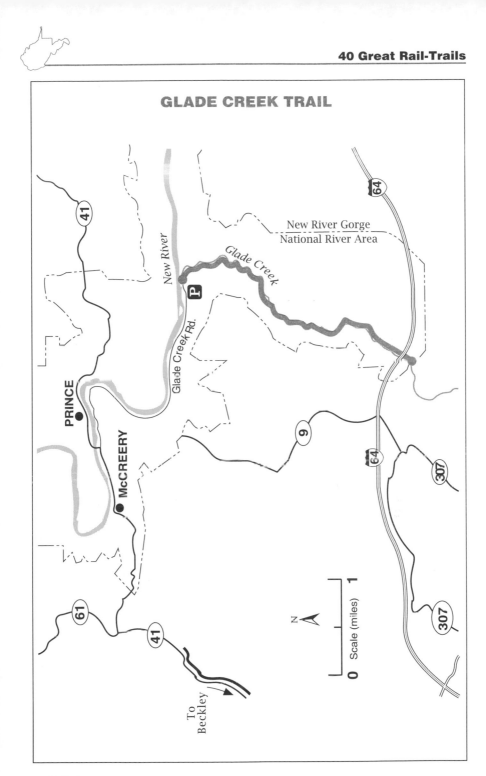

GLADE CREEK TRAIL

Beckley. There you will find numerous maps and detailed information on activities available in the New River Gorge. Unfortunately, the visitors' center is only open Monday through Friday.

To reach the trail's access road from the headquarters, take State Route 61 about 7.5 miles south to State Route 41 south. Continue four miles to the Glade Creek Access Road, located on the west side of the New River, prior to the bridge crossing into Prince. (You may want to cross the bridge just to see the exceptional views of the New River and the sizable gorge.)

The 5.5-mile dirt access road includes one creek crossing, which is usually shallow and passable in the summer. However, if you don't have a four-wheel drive vehicle, you may want to check conditions with the Park Service before attempting to reach the trailhead.

Traveling down this road gives you a clear idea of the gorge you are entering. Trees shroud most of the road and magnificent mountains loom all around you. Once you reach the base of the New River, you will find more spectacular views, plenty of parking, picnic tables and a recently-developed camping area with about a dozen sites. The area surrounding the trailhead is the site of the former town of Hamlet, which once had nearly 30 homes, a post office, a three-story clubhouse and a doctor's office. All of this had

This foot bridge over Glade Creek signals the trail's halfway mark.

sprung up to support the area's sawmill. When it closed during the Depression, the town disbanded. Today, it's hard to imagine that any of these structures ever existed given the pristine, densely shaded area where the only sound is the pleasant rippling of Glade Creek.

You will feel the trail's moderate ascent almost immediately. You may also be surprised that the trail is somewhat curvy compared to many other flat and straight rail-trails. This is because narrow gauge railroads were not built to the same stringent requirements as traditional freight railroads. The swishing creek on your left is one of the few sounds you'll hear as you travel along the route.

Just before the one-mile mark, you will come to an overlook of the creek, followed almost immediately by a gorgeous waterfall. At this point, you need to scramble up a few steps, and soon you will see a pile of railroad ties—one of the few remaining relics of the route's heritage. Within 0.8 miles, the trail briefly levels out and you pass a series of pools in the creek. Fishing is a popular activity along the creek, which is stocked with trout several times a year.

By the two-mile mark, you will be scrambling around some more rocks, the result of rockslides in the area, and you will hear more waterfalls off to the left. Take some time to enjoy the rushing water. Next, you will pass through an area where white-tailed deer are often visible from the trail. The area surrounding the trail is also home to many animals including deer, black bear, wild turkey, foxes and bobcat.

You are more than halfway up the trail when you come to an arched foot bridge that crosses Glade Creek almost exactly three miles from the trailhead. Unless otherwise signed, primitive camping is allowed in the areas surrounding the trail, which connects to several additional hiking trails in another 1.5 miles. The Kates Falls Trail branches left off the Glade Creek Trail just beyond the 4.5-mile mark. And, the Kates Falls Trail offers access to the Plateau Trail and the Poles Plateau Trail.

You will know you are nearing the trail's end when you pass under the massive steel bridge of Interstate 64. Interestingly, you will barely hear the traffic until you are practically under the bridge. If you are in the mood to take a dip in Glade Creek, the two sizable swimming holes under the bridge may appeal to you. The end of this satisfying trail is marked with a gate.

Greenbrier River Trail

Endpoints: Cass to North Caldwell

Location: Pocahontas and Greenbrier Counties

Length: 75 miles

Surface: Original ballast, made of mostly hard-packed gravel

Uses:

Contact: Gil Willis, President
Greenbrier River Trail Association
Highway 219
Slaty Fork, WV 26291
304-572-3771

Danny Talbot
Assistant Superintendent
Watoga State Park
Marlinton, WV 24954
304-799-4087

◆◆◆

If you want to experience the true "Wild, Wonderful West Virginia," head to the Greenbrier River Trail. The spectacular wilderness of the Monongahela National Forest serves as the trail's predominant setting. And virtually the entire length parallels the Greenbrier River—the longest, free-flowing river in the eastern United States.

Construction of the Greenbrier Division of the C&O Railroad was completed at the turn of the century to serve the booming timber

GREENBRIER RIVER TRAIL

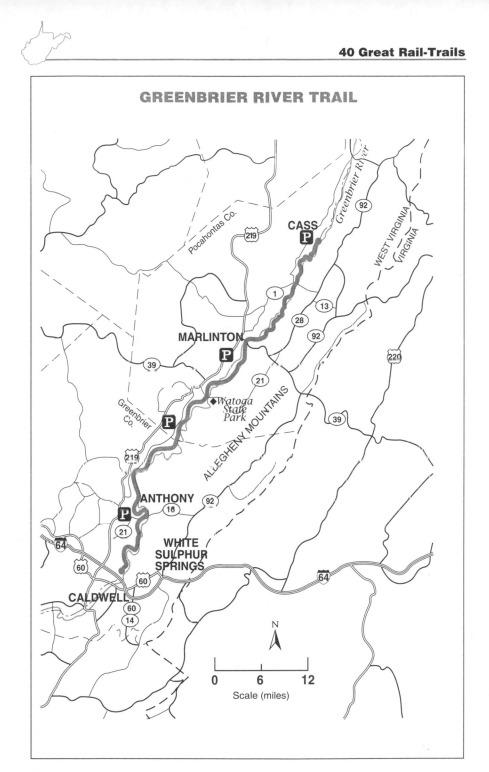

N

0   6   12

Scale (miles)

Frank Proud

This original railraod mileage marker sits near the middle of the Greenbrier River Trail.

industry. The corridor, abandoned in 1978, was part of a 3,000-mile statewide system of logging railroads. The C&O Railroad donated the line to the state of West Virginia, which has been operating it as a trail since 1980.

While the trail's mileage markers originate at its southern terminus, the grade will be in your favor if you travel from north to south as outlined in this description.

The Greenbrier River Trail is a true wilderness trail, so plan to carry ample food and water. Limited services are available only in a few towns and parks along the route. Currently, about 10 primitive campsites have been developed along the trail, with additional camping available in the Monongahela National Forest and at nearby Watoga State Park, Greenbrier State Forest, Seneca State Forest and Bluestone Recreation Area.

You can get to the northern end of the Greenbrier River Trail from Cass Scenic Railroad State Park, where you can ride into yesteryear on a steam locomotive that climbs Cheat Mountain—West Virginia's second highest peak. The awesome sight of huge smoke clouds and the ear-piercing sound of the train whistle combine to make the start to your rail-trail adventure unforgettable. Within the

State Park, you will also find the Cass General Store, timber company houses restored as tourist accommodations, food and other supplies. Nearby Snowshoe Mountain Resort and the Elk River Touring Center in Slaty Fork offer lodging, bike rentals and guided bike tours.

To get to Cass, take State Route 28/92 south approximately 10 miles from U.S. Route 250; head west on State Route 66 to the park. Overnight parking is allowed here, but camping is not. The trail corridor begins just across from the Cass General Store. You will see that railroad tracks are in place at this point, so you need to walk or bike about a half-mile on Main Street to Deer Creek Road, where the surfaced trail begins.

Heading south from Cass, located at milepost 80, the first few miles are a bit rough, with some washouts. Use caution in this area. About 5.5 miles from Cass, you will pass through Stony Bottom, where you'll find a quaint motel and soft drink machines—your last chance to get a drink on the trail for nearly 20 miles.

In the next few miles you will cross over a meandering creek on several trestles. The largest one is located just before Clover

Frank Proud

Hikers and bicyclists are likely to see people canoeing on the Greenbrier River.

Linda Hanlon

This old water tank—the only one still standing on the Greenbrier corridor—offers insight into the trail's heritage.

Lick, near milepost 71. The C&O Depot at Clover Lick has been removed for restoration; it will be returned to its former site when the restoration is complete. Limited parking is available at Clover Lick, where County Road 1/4 provides access across the river to Seneca State Forest.

Continuing on the trail, the next few miles are pleasantly scenic with many wild ferns lining the trail and abundant wildlife throughout the area. If you stay alert, you may see a deer, a beaver or even a black snake. About five miles south of Clover Lick, you

can't miss Sharp's Tunnel and Bridge. Built in 1900, these highlights are the most photographed attractions on the Greenbrier River Trail. Just south of milepost 66, the trail runs through a darkened stone tunnel for 511 feet and emerges onto a 229-foot bridge 30 feet above the scenic Greenbrier River.

Climbing high on the east bank of the river, the trail bends southward through forests and farms. A campsite is located on the east side of the trail, south of milepost 64. The railroad's last remaining water tank, built in 1923, stands about 7.5 miles south of the campsite.

The wilderness of the Greenbrier River Trail soon gives way to the town of Marlinton. A bright red caboose and the adjacent red and yellow depot, built in 1901, welcome visitors. This beautifully restored depot near milepost 56 now serves as the Pocahontas County Tourist Information Center. Marlinton is a quaint and friendly place offering restaurants, groceries and lodging.

Just south of Marlinton, beyond milepost 56, is Knapp's Creek Bridge. It connects to Stillwell Park, where camping is available. The next several miles pass through forests and fields, and magnificent wildflowers line the route in spring and summer. Several trestles also help keep the trail interesting. An access area with parking is located in Buckeye, near milepost 52.

About four miles south of Buckeye, before you reach milepost 48, you can see ruins of the old town of Watoga. A close look on the trail's left side reveals the remains of a bank safe. In another mile, you will switch from the Greenbrier River's east side to its west side on the Watoga Bridge.

In about two miles, you will reach the town of Seebert. You can access nearby Watoga State Park and Calvin Price State Forest across the bridge, where you will find food, water and phones. Camping is available in Watoga State Park, the oldest and one of the largest state parks in West Virginia. Chestnut log and stone cabins built in the 1930s are tucked away in 10,000 forested acres. This area also marks the trail's halfway point.

Watoga State Park and Calvin Price State Forest parallel the river and the trail for most of the 7.5 miles to Beard. Located near the 38.5 mile mark, Beard offers trail access, parking and a charming bed-and-breakfast called The Current.

The next several miles are among the most remote on the trail. The views on the left of the Greenbrier River Trail are spectacular,

Linda Hanlon

Sharp's Tunnel and Bridge is one of the most-photographed sections of the Greenbrier River Trail.

while steep hills line the right side. A few campsites have been developed over the next several miles. The trail's second tunnel, Droop Mountain Tunnel, is located just south of milepost 31. A relatively short tunnel at 402 feet, it looks much longer (and darker) until you get inside and can see around the bend.

An area known as Horrock, just south of milepost 30, offers trail access and parking. A campsite is located along the trail, less than two miles south of Horrock. The next hamlet is Rennick, where an asphalt road crosses the trail and a bridge crosses the Greenbrier River.

The 10-mile stretch between Rennick, located at the 24.5-mile mark, and Anthony is truly magnificent. A lush hardwood canopy bound by steep mountains borders the trail. There are several spots where you can get off the trail and hop across the cool waters of the Greenbrier River. The sight and sound of rushing water across huge rocks and the serenity of the surrounding wilderness are spellbinding.

Near milepost 14, the town of Anthony offers parking and trail access. You can also camp near the river and across the Greenbrier River Bridge on the Anthony Creek Trail. The Bluestone Recreation Area is located a few miles uphill from the Anthony trailhead.

Spectacular scenery along the Greenbrier River continues through the final stretch of trail from Anthony to Caldwell. You will pass through dense woods, rocky cliffs and open fields. This is a popular area because it can be reached by several county roads. You are likely to see many people tubing and fishing on warm summer days.

The southern trailhead at Caldwell has parking, picnic tables and drinking water. It is located 1.3 miles north of U.S. Route 60 on County Route 38 (Stonebridge Road). You can camp at nearby Greenbrier State Forest, located two miles east on Route 60. If it's a clear evening, you won't want to miss the million-star setting through the forest canopy of the Greenbrier State Forest—a perfect ending to one of the longest rail-trails in the east.

Future plans call for linking the Greenbrier River Trail's northern end with the West Fork Trail (see page 213) on the abandoned rail corridor that directly links the two. The state of West Virginia already owns the 20-mile gap between Cass and Durbin. When the connection takes place, West Virginia will be home to the nation's second longest rail-trail.

North Bend Rail-Trail

Endpoints: Wilsonburg to Walker

Location: Harrison, Doddridge, Ritchie and Wood Counties

Length: 60 miles

Surface: hard-packed crushed limestone in model sections; original ballast (ranging from loose gravel to large, chunky ballast) on all other sections

Uses:

         on model sections

Contact: Donnie Oates
North Bend Rail-Trail
Route 1, Box 220
Cairo, WV 26337
304-643-2931

◆◆◆

The North Bend Rail-Trail may be one of the nation's few trails that practically requires a flashlight. With 10 tunnels along the route—including four that are longer than 1,000 feet and one that's nearly a half-mile—you can spend a lot of time in the dark if you leave your flashlight at home. Of course you would still enjoy the spectacular mountain scenery, the occasional small towns and the rugged wilderness that surround this exceptional rail-trail.

Built by the Baltimore and Ohio Railroad between 1853 and 1857, the 60-mile railroad corridor between Wilsonburg and Walker

NORTH BEND RAIL-TRAIL

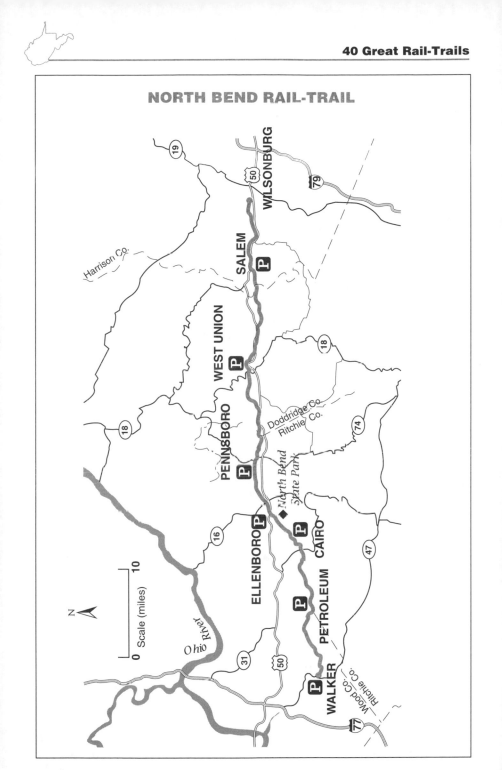

was extremely difficult to build because of the rugged, mountainous terrain. With the help of more than 20 tunnels and nearly 50 bridges, the B&O mainline finally opened. Over the years, the line serviced the lumber, coal and petroleum industries and also transported passengers. The CSX Corporation abandoned the rail line in the late 1980s, when the volunteer-led North Bend Rails-to-Trails Foundation launched the trail effort.

The trail's eastern terminus is located in the town of Wilsonburg, but access is limited on the far eastern end. The best place to get onto the trail is Salem, where the trail cuts through the center of town. Located just south of U.S. Route 50 on State Route 23, Salem is more than 200 years old. The town is brimming with Victorian architecture, and you will see a refurbished B&O caboose and depot. Restaurants, a grocery store, a gas station, an antique shop and a bank are nearby. Trail parking is located near the intersection of East Main and South Street.

One of the trail's four model sections heads east from Salem for nearly four miles. The state has developed a short section of trail in each county, paving the trail with limestone and posting signs. It's worth traveling this model section to get a feel for what the future holds for the North Bend Rail-Trail—and to see one of the trail's longer tunnels.

About 3.5 miles toward Wilsonburg, after crossing under Route 50, you will come to the 1,086-foot-long Tunnel #2. This imposing structure is one of the few straight tunnels on the trail. If you've brought a flashlight, now is the time to use it. A headlight for your bike or a strap-on headlamp could prove even more helpful. Once on the other side of the tunnel, the developed portion of the trail soon ends. You can travel on the rough surface for nearly three miles, although there's little to see. The trail ends anti-climactically near Wilsonburg.

When you head west from Salem, the trail parallels Main Street through town. The model section ends at the edge of town, and the trail surface is extremely rough for the next four miles. If you're on a bike and don't mind getting rattled, you can stay on the trail. Otherwise, ride on the parallel road. The surroundings get progressively more rural and scenic. And about 4.5 miles from Salem, you can see an abandoned tunnel (formerly Tunnel #3) on the trail's north side.

Karen-Lee Ryan

Tunnels, such as this brick-lined one in Ritchie County, are a dominant force in the North Bend Rail-Trail.

The next section of trail is still rough, but less so than the last few miles. You may want to get back on the trail because in less than a mile, you will come to Long Run Tunnel (#4) named for the creek that parallels the trail here. This relatively short tunnel is followed by a series four railroad bridges in about three miles. The fourth bridge is the only one with wood decking and handrails. This section of trail is mostly wooded, with many sycamores lining the corridor.

You will pass under Route 50 again before coming into the town of Smithburg, where an old depot has been restored. This attractive red building signals the start of the Doddridge County model section, which extends about four miles. You will notice steep walls of rock lining the trail intermittently, and a creek running along the trail's right side. Its quietly rippling waters help diminish the traffic sounds from Route 50, which towers high above the trail.

This section includes three bridges, all of which have decking and handrails. The trail's longest bridge crosses over State Route 18 and Middle Island Creek as you head into the town of West Union. The trail cuts below Main Street, although you can get up to

the street easily. In town you will find ample parking, a convenience store, several shops and eateries and some noteworthy Victorian architecture.

Once you are on the edge of town, the trail resumes its rugged surface. You will cross over Old Route 50 on a primitive bridge before coming to one of the trail's most stunning features: a 2,297 foot long tunnel (#6), the longest on the trail. The tunnel is so long that it is difficult to see any light coming from the other end despite the tunnel's straightness. Inside, the tunnel stays cool all summer and often has standing water on the bumpy surface.

Soon after exiting the tunnel, you will cut directly in front of the few homes that constitute the town of Central Station. The trail again parallels Route 50, heading toward Greenwood, although the trail ducks behind some rocky outcroppings before reaching the town. There's not much to see in Greenwood, although trail parking is available behind the West Virginia Department of Highways garage. (Take the Greenwood exit off of Route 50.)

Next you will pass quickly through the town of Tollgate, population 53, which is just about at the trail's mid-point. This town originally thrived around the timber industry and later became a hub for the oil industry with general stores, hotels, blacksmith shops, a hardware store, a church and a school. In the 1930s, Tollgate was the site of huge train wreck.

The surface continues to be bumpy through this section, where you will climb slightly until you reach the next tunnel. Tunnel #7 is curved, brick-lined and 779 feet long. The surface in the tunnel is rough and often covered with a significant amount of water, particularly on the western end.

You will make a slight descent into Pennsboro, where family restaurants and a feed store are located near the trail. Several attractive Victorian homes are adjacent to the trail, which regains its rural tone outside Pennsboro. In less than a mile, you will approach Tunnel #8, another curved, brick-lined tunnel. At 588 feet, this is considered a short tunnel on the North Bend. The surface on the other side of the tunnel can be very muddy, making it hard to pedal if you are on a bike.

About a mile east of Ellenboro, you will pass a shooting range on the trail's left side, so use caution, especially during hunting season. Five miles from Pennsboro, you will pass through the

town of Ellensboro, where you can tour a hand-blown glass factory. Fortunately, a new bridge has been constructed over State Route 16, once a dangerous at-grade crossing for trail users. You will see a few eateries in the area, as well as a bike shop—the last services for several miles.

As you leave Ellenboro, you will pass the new Ritchie County High/Middle School complex just before crossing under U.S. Route 50. At this point, the surface becomes smoother and the surroundings more scenic. A creek runs off to the right before rock formations overshadow the trail from both sides.

Within another mile, you will arrive at the short (337 feet) but intriguing tunnel that has been dedicated to trail visionary Dick Bias. This tunnel, the first of three in two miles, was bored from solid rock and has a more natural, unfinished look than some of the previous tunnels. The first of several picnic tables is located at the other end.

Soon you will approach the 577-foot-long Tunnel #12. Less than a half-mile later, you will reach Tunnel #13, which is the start of Ritchie County's model section. The smooth, dry surface inside this tunnel signals what the future holds for the other tunnels as the trail is further developed in the coming years. Outside, a picnic table and information kiosk have been placed just before a bridge crossing Bonds Creek. A map on the kiosk shows how to reach the nearby North Bend State Park, which offers camping and a wide variety of recreational activities.

Within a mile, you will pass through the historic town of Cornwallis. Once home to 250 people, only three families remain in the town that served the timber and oil industries over the years. You can find many ruins in the town, including an old Methodist church and the former two-story Marsh Brothers store. Along the 3.5-mile model section, you will cross the North Fork of the Hughes River on several refurbished bridges and pass abandoned Tunnel #17 on the trail's north side about two miles beyond Tunnel 13.

The surrounding landscape gets progressively more mountainous, and soon the trail skirts a wall of rocks on the left side. This model section may have some of the trail's most striking scenery.

As you head into the tiny town of Cairo, you are likely to see remnants of the petroleum industry that once fueled growth in this area. Oil was discovered in the area in 1890, and at the turn of the

Jane Whitaker

The pastoral town of Tollgate mark's the mid-section of the 60-mile North Bend Rail-Trail.

century the town bustled with an opera house, three hotels, two railroads, a newspaper and more. Today you will find a couple of restaurants and gift shops, and a bike shop that offers rentals. This shop was one of the first businesses to open up along the trail, which has since prompted nearly 20 new establishments geared toward trail users. Plenty of parking is available close to the trail.

From Cairo west, the trail gets decidedly more remote and rugged. The surface returns to chunky ballast, an unwelcome change after the smooth limestone, particularly since the trail heads steadily uphill for the next few miles. The spectacular scenery diverts your attention from the incline, and a little more than three miles west of Cairo, you will reach the third longest tunnel on the trail.

Known as the Silver Run Tunnel, this 1,376-foot brick-lined tunnel has a spirited history. In the past, many railroad crews claimed to have seen a phantom woman in a flowing white dress just outside the tunnel on foggy nights. While she does not seem to have made any recent appearances, the story adds an element of intrigue as you enter the curved tunnel in a darkness that seems impenetrable even with a flashlight.

Economic Development

When the CSX Corporation decided to abandon its rail line between Wilsonburg and Walker, it was another economic strike against an area that had already experienced dramatic declines in the coal, petroleum and lumber industries. Resourceful local citizens did not focus on their latest loss. Instead they shifted their energy to promoting the economic opportunities of a 60-mile rail-trail.

Focusing primarily on tourism-generated income, the North Bend Rails-to-Trails Foundation has encouraged trail-related businesses to open in the small towns along the route. The organization even convinced several local banks to offer low-interest loans to individuals interested in revamping an existing trail business or starting a new one.

The program is clearly working. To date, 20 new businesses have sprung up along the trail, including several bike shops, a handful of trailside restaurants and two gift shops. In addition, the trail's first bed-and-breakfast is scheduled to open in mid-1995.

As word travels throughout the recreation community that the North Bend Rail-Trail is an enchanting destination, the demand for additional business should increase. In the end, everyone wins: trail users will have access to important services, and trailside communities will experience and economic boost.

Next, you will head downhill toward the town of Petroleum, once a bustling industrial area. Before you get there, however, you will need to negotiate a couple of unimproved bridges. Hiking with caution and walking your bike are obvious precautions on these Goose Creek crossings that have large gaps and missing ties. You will see many relics of the oil industry as you briefly pass through the now-small town of Petroleum, where a bed and breakfast is scheduled to open in spring of 1995. In its heyday, Petroleum boasted two general stores, a hotel, two churches and a post office—one of the few buildings still standing.

From here, you are about seven miles from the trail's western end at Walker. The surface remains rough, and you have several more unfinished and occasionally nerve-wracking bridges to cross. You are also making one of the trail's steeper climbs. About four miles west of Petroleum (two of which are uphill), you reach Eaton Tunnel, the trail's second longest at 1,840 feet. While this tunnel signals Wood County's three-mile model section, the surface inside is somewhat bumpy. Hopefully, the batteries in your flashlight are still working!

Once outside the tunnel, you will begin your descent into the town of Walker on the smooth crushed limestone surface. You will pass another abandoned tunnel as the scenery around you seems to flatten out. You will reach the western trailhead in Walker, nearly 54 miles from Salem and almost exactly 60 miles from Wilsonburg.

Karen-Lee Ryan

This rock slide has taken up permanent residence on the Thurmond to Minden Trail.

Thurmond to Minden Trail

Endpoints: Thurmond to Minden within the New River
Gorge National River area

Location: Fayette County

Length: 3.2 miles

Surface: Dirt and gravel

Uses:

Contact: Superintendent
National Park Service
New River Gorge National River
P.O. Box 246
Glen Jean, WV 25846
304-465-0508

◆◆◆

While on the short side, the Thurmond to Minden Trail packs in some interesting geological formations and offers excellent views of the historic—and now deserted—town of Thurmond and the New River Gorge. Well-suited for families with young children, this rail-trail can be worked into a longer and more rigorous outing by combining it with other trails in the New River Gorge area.

Completed in 1904, the Arbuckle Branch of the C&O Railroad was built to haul coal from Minden to Thurmond. Millions of tons of coal were hauled by steam engines over the years. The line was abandoned during the 1970s, and a local hiking club encouraged its conversion into a trail. In 1978, the National Park Service got involved after it began managing the New River Gorge National River. Hard-working volunteers assured the route's conversion into a trail.

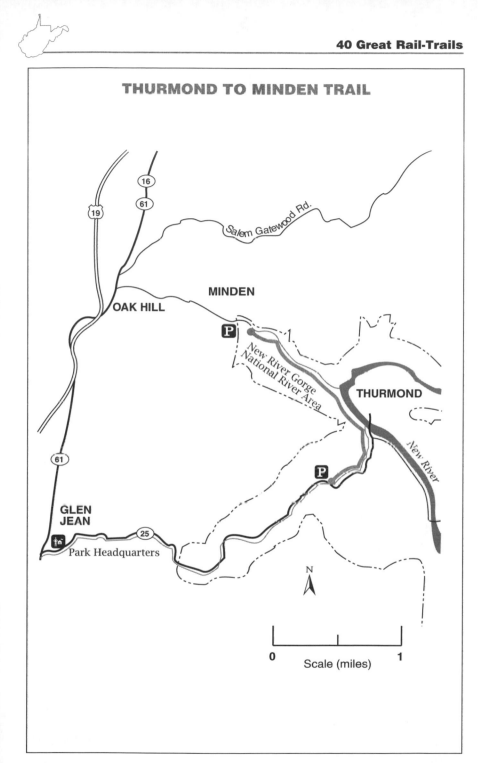

THURMOND TO MINDEN TRAIL

You may want to begin your trip on the Thurmond to Minden Trail with a stop at the New River Gorge National River Headquarters in Glen Jean. The office, which unfortunately has no weekend hours, offers excellent trail information and specific ideas for linking two or more trails together to make a longer trip.

To reach the Thurmond to Minden trailhead, take the Glen Jean/Thurmond exit off of West Virginia State Route 19 and go a half-mile to Glen Jean. Turn right onto Route 25 and bear left over the bridge. Then go 5.1 miles to the trailhead on the left side of the road.

Once you have maneuvered around (or under) the gate that marks the trail's beginning, you will pass the only portable toilet available on the trail. The grade is gentle at the outset as the trail parallels a pleasant creek. In less than half a mile, you may come to what looks like a fork in the trail caused by occasional work crews in the area—bear to the left even if it looks more traveled on the right side.

The uphill grade becomes more noticeable after the "fork," and the chunky surface mimics the railroad ties that once covered the

Karen-Lee Ryan

Some of the bridges on the Thurmond to Minden Trail have not yet been fully decked for bicyclists.

trail. After a mile, you will reach the first—and longest—of the trail's five bridges. Bicyclists are urged to walk bikes over the bridges because they lack handrails and include only minimal decking. When you get a glimpse of the steep drop-off to the right, you'll be more likely to heed the advice. Bridge improvements should be completed during 1995.

Shortly after the bridge, you will come to two overlooks of Thurmond, which is on the opposite side of the New River. The Park Service is restoring the old railroad depot (scheduled for a spring 1995 opening) and providing interpretive information for this town, which should attract more visitors to the area.

Next, you will come to the trail's most intriguing and challenging feature: a rockslide that has taken permanent residence on the corridor. While there seems to be little documentation of when the rockslide happened, some people believe it may have played a role in the railroad's abandonment. Take a moment to get the best views of Thurmond before undertaking the scramble around the rockslide—it can be quite cumbersome with a bike.

The breathtaking views of the New River occur at the next overlook, immediately before the second bridge. This overpass, like the third one, is quite short. Between these two bridges, many of railroad ties remain on the corridor. Although the trail actually falls to the right of the ties, it makes for an interesting diversion to ride on top of them for a short distance.

As you ease your way uphill toward Minden, thousands of rhododendrons line the trail. When they bloom, usually in early July, they add an enchanting dimension to an already appealing setting.

The trail's fourth bridge is longer than the previous two and is more interesting because of its curve. Interestingly, the fifth bridge, which signals your final ascent into Minden, is fully decked and has handrails. This may be a sign of future development of this trail, as its usage steadily increases.

A number of original railroad relics remain on the trail, including the whistlepost near the top of the trail. This metal sign with a simple "W" signaled engineers to blow their whistle at this point to alert townspeople of their approach.

Another gate marks the trail's end. If you are turning around at this point, you may be amazed at how fast your return trip will be. The trail has a subtle grade for its entire length, and you will notice (and appreciate) it on your way down.

West Fork Trail

Endpoints: Greenbrier Junction to Durbin

Location: Pocahontas and Randolph Counties

Length: 25.5 miles

Surface: Original ballast

Uses:

Contact: Jim Thomas, District Ranger
Greenbrier Ranger District
Monongahela National Forest
P.O. Box 67
Bartow, WV 24920
304-456-3335

◆◆◆

Have you ever witnessed the birth of a river? On the West Fork Trail you'll see a small stream become a spectacular river that winds its way through a rich array of ecosystems brimming with wildlife. Beaver ponds, marshes, hardwood forests, white-tailed deer, migrating ducks and geese and some of the best fishing in West Virginia are all part of the adventure on the West Fork Trail.

The former rail line was constructed by the Coal and Iron Railway Company in the early 1900s, and was later sold to the Western Maryland Railway Company. Coal, timber and passengers were transported on the corridor. Then, following abandonment, the Trust for Public Land purchased the corridor and then sold it to the U.S. Forest Service in 1986.

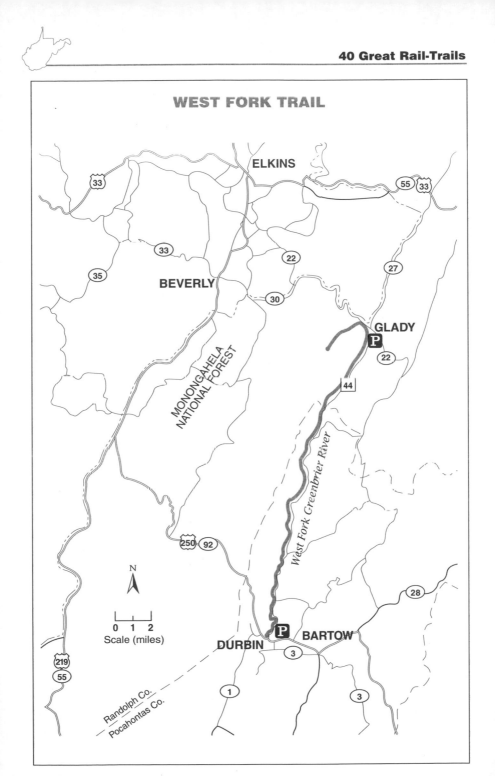

WEST FORK TRAIL

ELKINS

33

55 33

33

22

35

27

BEVERLY

30

GLADY
P
22

MONONGAHELA
NATIONAL FOREST

44

West Fork Greenbrier River

250 92

N

28

0 1 2
Scale (miles)

P
DURBIN
3
BARTOW

219

55

1

3

Randolph Co.
Pocahontas Co.

Carol Parker

This attractive depot at Durbin has been restored and now serves as a community center for this small town.

Primarily located in the Greenbrier Ranger District of the Monongahela National Forest, the West Fork Trail does pass through private land in the Glady area. Camping is available on the public lands surrounding much of the route; the Greenbrier Ranger District can provide information.

The West Fork Trail remains a rugged and remote trail, with no facilities along the way. The surface is dirt and gravel, and the trail's original trestles are in place but not decked. Bicyclists may want to walk their bikes and equestrians may opt to detour through streams.

The West Fork Trail is shaped like an upside down fishhook. The long shank of the hook parallels the north-flowing West Fork of Glady Fork, which is entwined with the south-flowing West Fork of the Greenbrier River. The hook's curved end serves as the trail's western terminus at Greenbrier Junction, an isolated railroad junction located along the beautiful Shavers Fork River about four miles southwest of Glady.

Since Greenbrier Junction is not accessible by car, plan to begin your journey at the trail's northern-most point in Glady. From there, you can hike or bicycle to Greenbrier Junction. To get to the

access area in Glady, take U.S. Route 33 east from Elkins to Alpena. Turn south onto County Road 27, located across from the historic Alpine Lodge, and travel about nine miles to Glady. The trail is located near the center of town, where on-street parking is available.

No formal trailheads have been constructed along the West Fork Trail. However, in addition to easy access at Glady and at the trail's southern terminus in Durbin, you can get onto the trail from several points along West Fork Road. This is Forest Service Road 44, and it parallels the trail for most of its length.

Plan to explore the 3.8 miles between Glady and Greenbrier Junction even though it means retracing your steps. If you head this way, you will come to a tunnel within about a mile, which is often saturated with ankle-deep water even in the summer. Avoid the tunnel during winter because it can be dangerously icy and filled with huge icicles. A detour is possible by using County Road 27 and County Road 22. In less than two miles, you will pass Cheat Junction. This is where the former railroad divided. Today the area is surrounded by hardwood forest, where several primitive campsites are available. The trail ends in less than a mile.

The main portion of the trail extends due south from Glady, where a small country store, which doubles as the town's post office, is open during daylight hours. As you head south, you soon will pass a small graveyard on the left. The scenery for the next several miles is rustic, with sheep and cattle grazing on pasture lands.

About 3.5 miles south of Glady, the trail intersects with the High Falls Trail about a half-mile west of Forest Service Road 44. In a little more than two miles, you need to look closely to detect the trail's crossing of the north/south watershed of Glady Fork and the Greenbrier River. Watch for the hillsides pinching together—this is where the Lynn Divide forms. Here, rain falling to the north of the divide flows to the city of Morgantown via the Cheat River and eventually to Pittsburgh and into the Ohio River. Rain falling south of the divide flows to Lewisburg by way of the Greenbrier River and then to Charleston, via the New and Kanawha Rivers.

The scenery is splendidly beautiful—although not especially varied—throughout the trail's remaining 16 miles. Along this stretch of trail, you will see a nearby small stream transform into a respectable river, which attracts plentiful wildlife. You will cross the river

Frank Proud

Fresh snow falls on the rural West Fork Trail, attracting plenty of users, including backpackers and cross-country skiers.

several times on the old railroad trestles. You might also want to venture into the river, which has many deep, clear swimming holes.

After you pass under U.S. Route 250, nearly 22 miles south of Glady, you will reach the trail's southern terminus at Durbin. The town restored its beautiful Victorian depot, which now serves as a community center. Hours are limited, however. Parking is available at the depot, and groceries and phones are located in town.

About 20 miles south of Durbin, this same corridor has been converted into the 75-mile Greenbrier River Trail (see page 191). If West Virginia trail advocates get their way, the two trails may again form a continuous route someday.

An Introduction to Rail-Trails in Ohio

With more than 20 trails totaling 150 miles and another 50 rail-trail projects in the works, Ohio is rapidly taking shape as a leader in the rail-trail movement. And, citizens and agencies throughout Ohio are placing great emphasis on creating networks of trails that will connect communities, while preserving a piece of the Buckeye State's heritage.

In the early 20th century, Ohio's railroad mileage peaked at 9,148 miles. In recent years, more than 3,000 miles have been abandoned—2,300 of them since 1972.

The state's earliest rail-trails were created in the early 1970s, with new ones slowly opening up through the 1980s. In 1989, trail advocates throughout the state banded together to form the Ohio Chapter of Rails-to-Trails Conservancy. Based in Columbus, the Ohio Chapter is staffed by two people who provide technical assistance, educate the public on the benefits of rail-trails and build new coalitions throughout the state.

And now, the Ohio Chapter and other trail enthusiasts are rallying around an interconnected statewide system known as the Discover Ohio Trails System. This visionary network calls for linking the proposed 325-mile Ohio to Erie Trail, which will run from the Cincinnati Riverfront to the Cleveland Lakefront via Columbus, with four other regional trail systems to unite all four corners of the state.

This book highlights a small sample of this vast, emerging system. And whether your journeys take you to Cincinnati, Columbus, Cleveland or another part of Ohio, you will find interesting and enjoyable trail experiences.

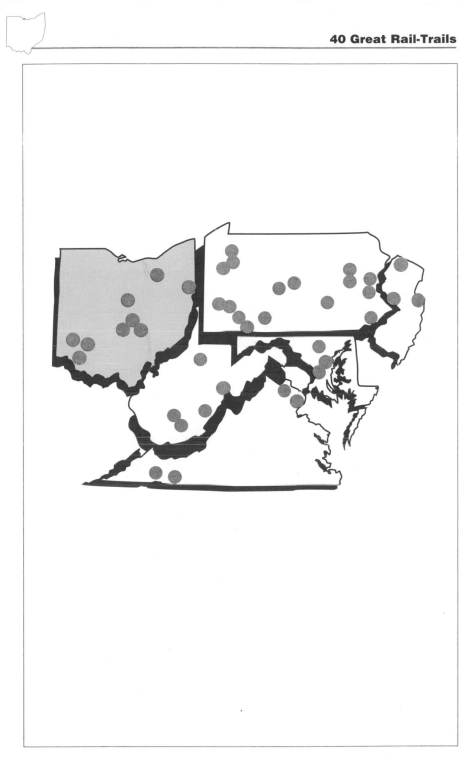

OHIO'S GREAT RAIL-TRAILS

1. Bike & Hike Trail

2. Blackhand Gorge Bikeway

3. Kokosing Gap Trail

4. Little Miami Scenic Trail

5. Little Miami State Park

6. Olentangy-Scioto Bikeway

7. Stavich Bicycle Trail

8. Thomas J. Evans Bike Trail

9. Wolf Creek Bikeway

The Bike & Hike Trail appeals to a broad range of users.

Seneca Murley

Bike & Hike Trail

Endpoints: Walton Hills to Kent and Stow

Location: Cuyahoga, Summit and Portage Counties

Length: 24 miles of a 28-mile trail are on abandoned railroad corridor

Surface: Crushed limestone and asphalt when on-street

Uses:

 on certain sections

Contact: Dave Whited, Chief of Planning
Metro Parks Serving Summit County
975 Treaty Line Road
Akron, OH 44313
216-867-5511

Steve Coles
Chief of Planning
Cleveland Metroparks
4101 Fulton Parkway
Cleveland, OH 44144
216-351-6300, ext. 238

Ohio's oldest rail-trails, the Bike & Hike Trail offers
an urban greenway between the outskirts of Cleveland and
Akron. This trail takes its roots from a couple of different railroads. The northern section began as the Pittsburgh and Lake
Erie Railroad, which later became the New York Central Railroad.
Most of the southern section was originally the Akron, Bedford and

BIKE & HIKE TRAIL

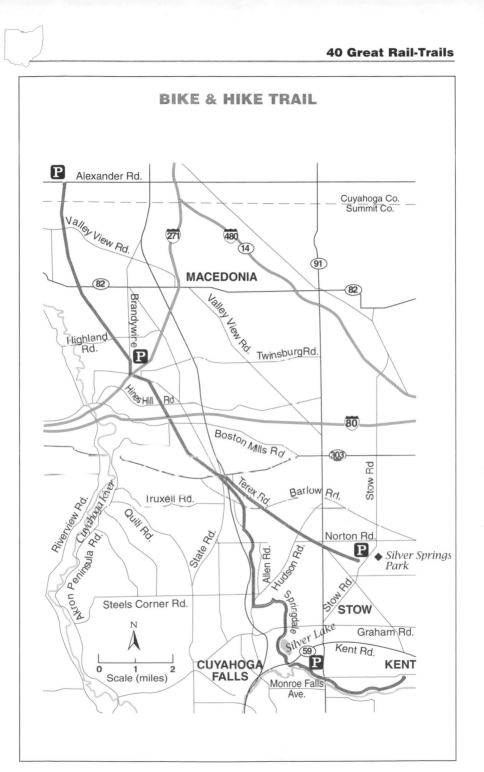

Cleveland Railroad, fondly referred to as the "Alphabet Railroad." This line served as a commuter railroad, carrying passengers between Akron and Cleveland. The Bike & Hike Trail opened in 1972.

To get to the northern trailhead, take State Route 14 west from Interstate 271 and proceed to Northfield Road (State Route 8). Go south on Northfield for about a mile to Alexander Road, where you will go west for more than a mile. A small trail parking lot is located at the intersection of Alexander and Dunham roads. A larger one is located about a half-mile west on Alexander Road.

If you park at the first lot, a trail that parallels Alexander Road for a half-mile leads you to the Bike & Hike Trail (surfaced with crushed limestone and gravel), which heads south on the former railroad grade. The Bedford Multi-Use Trail, managed by Cleveland Metroparks, also begins at the intersection of Alexander and Dunham roads. You can take it north into the Bedford Reservation, where you will find numerous picnic areas and shelters amid towering trees.

The first few miles of the Bike & Hike Trail are pleasant, although not overly scenic. High-tension power lines tower over the trail after the first road crossing at Sagamore Road. Fortunately,

Shawn Richardson

The Bike & Hike Trail offers a tree-lined setting for much of its length.

trees line the corridor, keeping the setting green throughout spring and summer and colorful in the fall. The National Park Service's Cuyahoga Valley National Recreation Area borders the trail's left side for the next several miles.

About 2.5 miles from Sagamore Road, you will cross busy State Route 82 at grade. Use caution. The next road crossing will be Holzhauer Road, where you can pick up the Ohio and Erie Canal Towpath Trail. To do so, turn right on Holzhauer and follow it to the end. Here, you will find a crushed stone path that leads steeply downhill to the Towpath Trail.

Less than a mile past Holzhauer Road, the power lines turn away from the Bike & Hike Trail, completely changing its atmosphere. Larger hardwoods arch over the trail and the hum of the power lines yields to a quiet serenity. The next two miles include a few road crossings.

Beyond the Highland Road crossing, about five miles from the start of the trail, the surface becomes smoother. This signals the start of the section managed by Akron Metro Parks, Serving Summit County. From this point south, you will pass through a cumbersome set of gates—with extremely narrow openings—at every road crossing. This poorly designed barrier may frustrate some bicyclists and makes wheelchair passage impossible. The gates farther south have been widened.

At Brandywine Road, where parking is available, the trail temporarily diverges from the railroad grade to reach a bridge over Interstate 271. This one-mile, unsigned detour takes you downhill on Brandywine Road, only to go back uphill to return to the trail. Just prior to crossing the highway, you can take a detour to Brandywine Falls, where restrooms and picnic tables are also located.

After crossing the Ohio Turnpike on the Bike & Hike Trail bridge, you will reach Boston Mills Road. A mile marker indicates that you have traveled three miles from Highland Road. Here you'll find a major access point with a map and parking.

As you continue south the trail remains densely wooded and the trail seems to sit atop a ridge. This area, known as Boston Ledges, is one of the trail's most scenic. The railroad made extensive cuts through this area, exposing huge rocks on either side of the trail. Wild ferns line the trail's edge, with occasional wildflowers adding color to the area.

The northern end of the Bike & Hike Trail.

Soon you will travel under State Route 303, signaling a turn away from the Cuyahoga Valley National Recreation area. Next you will travel up a ramp and cross over State Route 8. Just beyond this point, the trail forks. As the signs indicate, the leg heading southeast continues 5.5 miles to Silver Springs Park and the City of Stow. The southward leg ends at Munroe Falls in Kent after 11.4 miles.

The shorter segment, which is the newest section of the trail, offers a continuously green setting. Initially, you will head downhill and telephone lines soon parallel the route. Within about a mile, you will cross Truxell Road. At this point, you can see several new home developments through a thin veil of trees. You will cross over State Route 91 more than a mile from Silver Springs Park. The park is a pleasant spot, with expansive grassy areas and picnic tables. If you stay alert, you may see several types of birds in the area, including red-tailed hawks. The trail ends just beyond the park's eastern edge.

The section of the trail that leads to Munroe Falls is not for everyone. The first couple of miles remain on the former railroad corridor, but when the corridor begins paralleling State Route 8, the trail gets quite hilly. In the Crystal Lake area, the trail takes a 3.5-mile jaunt through various neighborhoods—none of which are

The Ohio and Erie Towpath Trail

Next time you are in the Cleveland or Akron area, plan to spend some time exploring the Cuyahoga Valley National Recreation Area (CVNRA). This 33,000-acre river valley park is tucked between two heavily populated and industrialized areas, but you would never know it once you enter its boundaries. The Cuyahoga River, the quaint New England-style towns and an array of recreational facilities—including an outdoor concert arena and ski slopes—are among the highlights. For the trail enthusiast, the 19.5-mile Ohio and Erie Towpath Trail may be the main attraction.

Following the remnants of the Ohio & Erie Canal, the trail is packed with canal relics and interpretive displays of the area's prehistoric sites and rich transportation heritage. Developed and maintained by the National Park Service, the Towpath Trail acts as a spine through the Recreation Areas, with numerous connections to other hiking and bridle paths. It also connects to the Akron Bike/Hike Trail at Holzhauer Road. ▶

School groups often take field trips to the Towpath Trail to learn the area's heritage.

The Ohio and Erie Towpath Trail, *cont.*

Covered with a hard-packed crushed limestone surface, the Towpath Trail's southern trailhead is at Indian Mound just north of Akron. Its northern trailhead is at Lock 39 at Rockside Road south of Cleveland. Funding has been allocated to extend the Towpath Trail in both directions. This significant regional trail is also the northern leg of the proposed Ohio to Erie Trail, a cross-state trail that will connect Cincinnati to Cleveland via Columbus.

A popular destination within the CVNRA is the historic town of Peninsula, where one of the Towpath Trail's major trailheads is located. In addition to restaurants, crafts stores and a bike shop, this town offers steam-engine train rides through the valley. A popular summer trip, called the Bike and Hike, allows passengers to carry their bikes on the train and ride back to their destination.

For more information, contact: Superintendent, Cuyahoga Valley National Recreation Area, 15610 Vaughn Road, Brecksville, OH 44141; 216-524-1497 or 800-445-9667.

---

flat. South of Silver Lake, the trail resumes as a separate path paralleling the Cuyahoga River.

If you do take the Munroe Falls fork, you will cross Seasons Road within a mile. The trail becomes wooded again, giving it a remote quality. This changes within another mile when you begin to parallel State Route 8, a six-lane highway. Despite the fact that you are next to a flat and straight highway, the trail goes up and down while making several curves. Sight distances are poor, so use caution.

In another mile, you cross Steels Corners Road—a busy road that can be difficult to cross. Soon you will go on-street, crossing Hudson Drive. You will travel on Springdale Road for nearly a mile. Next, you will follow bike route signs through a cumbersome series of residential streets: Goldfinch Trail, Whipporwill Trail, Meadowlark Trail, Hummingbird Trail, Leewood Drive, Graham Road, North Dover and Highland, which turns into Silver Lake

Boulevard. This road skirts around Silver Lake, which offers a pleasant change of scenery.

Soon after crossing Kent Road, a separate trail resumes, continuing through Silver Lake Recreational Area, where a playground, picnic tables, a baseball diamond and portable toilets are located. You will cut between several new housing developments before reaching the parking lot at Darrow Road. Here you will find a gazebo and portable toilets.

The trail ends two miles east of this parking lot at North River Road in Kent. This section is quite scenic. It parallels the Cuyahoga River, where you might see great blue herons or Canada geese, for the rest of its length.

Blackhand Gorge Bikeway

Endpoints: Within the Blackhand Gorge Nature Preserve near Toboso

Location: Licking County

Length: 4 miles

Surface: Asphalt

Uses:

Contact: William Daehler
Division of Natural Areas and Preserves
Ohio Department of Natural Resources
Fountain Square
Columbus, OH 43224
614-265-6395

◆◆◆

The Blackhand Gorge Trail packs an incredible number of interesting features into its four short miles. While you can cover the trail quickly, you may want to dedicate the better part of a day to explore the beauty and rich history of the entire Blackhand Gorge State Nature Preserve.

The 970-acre area was dedicated in 1975 to preserve the historic sandstone gorge. Over many thousands of years, the Licking River had carved the gorge, which was a key transportation route for native Americans and pioneers.

Hundreds of years ago, native Americans etched a large, dark hand-shaped petroglyph on a sandstone cliff face. Pioneers who later moved into the area heard many tales of the "black hand" that supposedly marked the boundary of a sacred native American

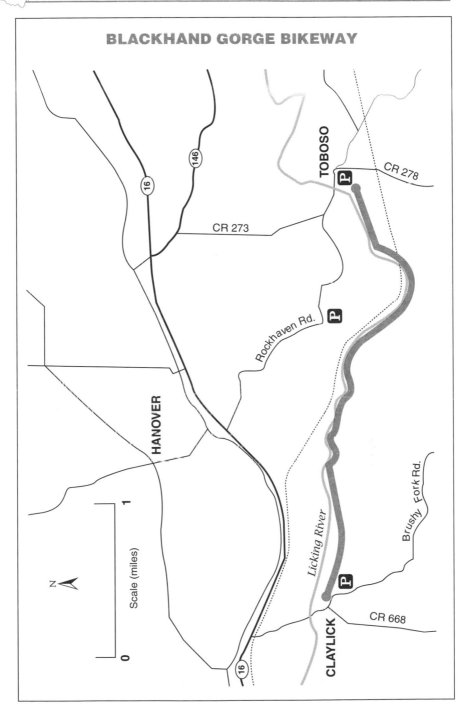

BLACKHAND GORGE BIKEWAY

territory, where no man was to raise a hand against another. Unfortunately, the image was destroyed during the construction of the Ohio to Erie Canal in 1828.

In addition to the canal, the Central Ohio Railroad operated steam trains through the gorge, and an electric interurban trolley cut through the area. All the transportation systems were abandoned before 1930, although a railroad still runs through the area on the opposite bank of the Licking River.

To reach the main entrance of the Nature Preserve, where the Blackhand Gorge Trailhead is located, take State Route 146 east from State Route 16. Follow the signs, and turn south onto County Road 273. You will see the park entrance in two miles. A small log cabin is located in the parking lot. There you can pick up a brochure that describes the area's history and you can get a map of all the trails within the park. Bathrooms are also located at the trailhead.

The trail is immediately surrounded by woodlands, and along the way you will see a mix of sycamore, cottonwood and box elder. In the summertime, the trail is refreshingly cool. The Quarry Rim

Linda Hanlon

An active set of railroad tracks crosses over the Blackhand Gorge Bikeway.

Linda Hanlon

The Blackhand Gorge attracts users of all ages.

Trail quickly heads off to the left and rejoins the Blackhand Gorge Trail in about a mile. Almost a half-mile from your starting point, you can take a short detour to the former site of "black hand" rock.

The Licking River is located to your right, but it is obscured by a steep sandstone rock formation that practically creates a tunnel on the trail. According to an interpretive sign on the trail, the Central Ohio Railroad Company created this 700 foot-long cut by using 1,200 kegs of black powder during the winter of 1851.

Soon, you will cross under the active railroad track as it makes its way across the Licking River. In a short distance, you will get your first glimpses of the river to your right, while dense woods parallel the trail's left side. The Owl Hollow Loop Trail and the Chestnut Trail—two hiking trails—veer off to the left near the 1.5-mile mark.

The trail remains densely wooded and scenic for the next mile, with wildflowers blooming during much of the spring and summer. Before mile three, you will need to ford a creek that is usually shallow in the summertime. The area on either side of the crossing is curvy and relatively steep, so use caution as you cross. Soon you will pass an open field off to the left, while the river continues to ripple along on your right.

Just beyond the 3.5 mile mark, the river bends away from the trail. Wildflowers take over the right edge of the corridor, while woods return to the left. In another half-mile, the trail bends left toward the western parking lot. Just before you get there, a portion of the trail continues straight. It ends abruptly, however, at County Road 668. A canoe launch area is located along the river, west of the county road.

If you have time, explore a few of the other trails in the Blackhand Gorge Nature Preserve. The three-quarter-mile Canal Lock Trail is developed on the corridor that was formerly the canal route before the interurban trolley operated along it. A short tunnel bored from solid rock makes the trail interesting.

The two trestles along the Kokosing Gap Trail remind users of the route's heritage.

Kokosing Gap Trail

Endpoints: Mount Vernon to Danville

Location: Knox County

Length: 14 miles

Surface: Asphalt

Uses: 🚶 🚲 ♿ 🛷 ⛷️

Contact: Phil Samuell, President
Board of Directors
Kokosing Gap Trail
P.O. Box 129
Gambier, OH 43022
614-427-4509 or 614-587-6267

◆ ◆ ◆

Cutting through rural central Ohio, the Kokosing Gap Trail offers a scenic respite from urban life within an hour's drive of downtown Columbus.

The Kokosing Gap Trail takes its roots from the Cleveland, Mt. Vernon and Columbus Railroad. Construction began in 1870 on this line that operated as a freight route with passenger service several times a day.

Later, the Pennsylvania Railroad took over the corridor, and Mt. Vernon quickly developed as a town to service the railroad. A trip between Cleveland and Mt. Vernon took about three hours, while traveling to Columbus took about an hour. The last passenger trains ran through the area in 1950. Conrail was the line's final operator, hauling sand from a nearby quarry a few times a week until 1982.

The Kokosing Gap Trail was dedicated in 1991, and its first 4.5 miles opened to the public. The Knox County Commissioners, who

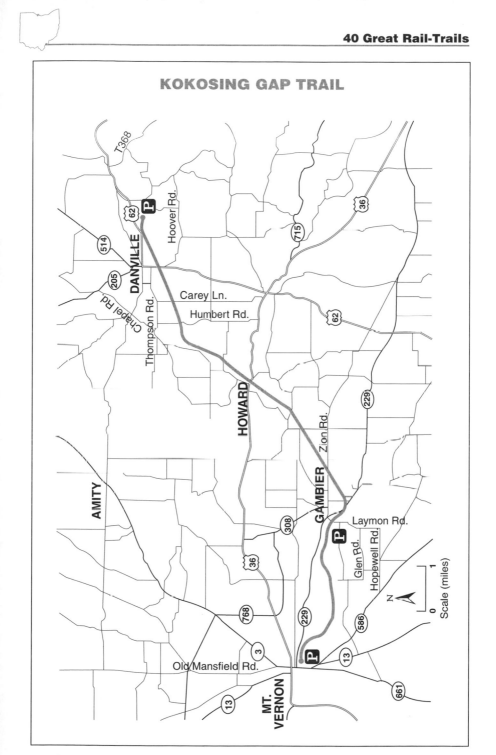

KOKOSING GAP TRAIL

Karen-Lee Ryan

A stone trestle near Howard is another highlight of the trail.

own and operate the trail, managed to acquire and develop another 9.5 miles of trail by mid-1994.

The Kokosing Gap Trail begins about a mile east of Mt. Vernon at the intersection of Mt. Vernon Avenue and Lower Gambier Road. Signs direct you to a large parking lot, where you will find information about the area's history. In 1808 John Chapman—popularly called Johnny Appleseed—planted an apple orchard near the trailhead.

Paved with asphalt, the trail is surrounded by hardwoods that give the trail a sheltered feeling. In less than 1.5 miles, you will cross over the Kokosing River on the trail's first steel trestle. This eye-catching structure is nearly 300 feet long, and a pull-off area has been built at either end so you can stop to enjoy the views.

The river continues to parallel the trail's left side, while woodlands and wildflowers line the right. Within another two miles, views of the surrounding landscape open up as you cut through the outskirts of Gambier, where additional parking is located off of Laymon Road. Farmland envelops the trail's corridor, while rolling hills provide a panoramic backdrop.

Just beyond the four-mile mark, you will need to negotiate a busy crossing of State Route 229; use caution. Soon you will see Kenyon College off to your left, and at 4.5 miles you will arrive at the Gambier trailhead. A new depot has been constructed at the site, offering phones, drinking water, bathrooms and a kiosk that illustrates your location relative to the nearby town of Gambier.

The next several miles of trail are pleasantly unchanging. Rows of corn practically grow up to the trail's edge during summer, although the crops occasionally yield to patches of lightly rolling terrain.

At mile marker 9 you will pass through the hamlet of Howard, where an 1860 grain mill has been restored on the trail's left side. You will also pass through a historic stone arch that carries you under busy U.S. Route 36. The Kokosing River veers away from the trail at this point.

Soon a similar mix of farmland and rolling hills resume as you proceed toward Danville. Within five miles, you will reach the trail's northeastern endpoint—and another parking lot—near the town of Danville.

In the future, a third segment of the trail could be developed between Danville and the Holmes County line. And, planners in Holmes County are looking into developing a trail that would connect with the Kokosing Gap Trail.

Little Miami Scenic Trail

Endpoints: Xenia to Yellow Springs

Location: Greene County

Length: 9.7 miles

Surface: Asphalt

Uses:

      🏇 on certain sections

Contact: Charles E. Dressler, Director
Greene County Park District
651 Dayton-Xenia Road
Xenia, OH 45385
513-376-7440

◆◆◆

Greene County's Little Miami Scenic Trail is the quintessential multi-use trail. The route's physical design—a wide asphalt path flanked by grassy shoulders—encourages the entire gamut of non-motorized uses. And the trail is a wonderful recreation corridor, linking two parks, a nature preserve, a federally-designated scenic river and several rippling creeks. On a more practical level, people use the trail to travel between Xenia and Yellow Springs and to reach various community resources.

The original railroad corridor was constructed by the Little Miami Railroad in 1841 as part of an eventual Cincinnati to Sandusky route. The company operated the line until 1921, when it leased the property to the Pennsylvania Railroad. Rail service declined over the years, with the last train passing through Xenia in 1966.

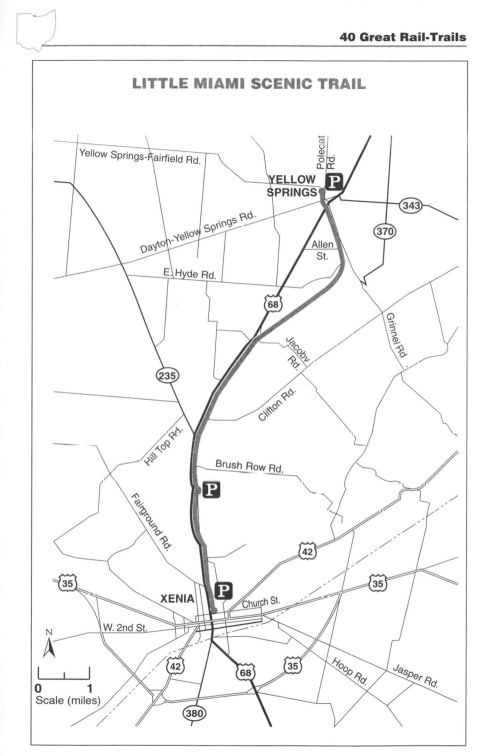

LITTLE MIAMI SCENIC TRAIL

Greene County began acquiring the route (with the help of the Ohio Department of Natural Resources) in the early 1970s. Within two years, this trail should connect with the Little Miami State Park, which continues southwest to the Cincinnati suburbs (see page 245).

The trail currently begins in downtown Xenia at Church Street and North Detroit Avenue, one block north of the Greene County Courthouse and U.S Route 35 (Main Street). Plenty of parking is available 0.2 miles north in Shawnee Park. Here you will also find a fountain, a large pond, picnic tables, restrooms, bike racks and an informational kiosk in a pristine setting.

Running parallel to U.S. 68 for the first few miles, the trail passes through primarily residential areas until reaching the Old Town Reserve near the 2.5-mile mark. In this green setting, you will find picnic tables, shade shelters, ample parking and a portable toilet. A short distance ahead, you will cross over Old Town Creek on a short bridge span and over Masssie Creek about a mile

Charles E. Dressler

Equestrians and bicyclists enjoy sharing the Little Miami Scenic Trail.

later. By now the trail has begun to take on a more pastoral feeling with woodlands lining the left side and rolling hills off to the right.

Next, you will cross over the Little Miami Scenic River on a refurbished railroad trestle. While you are in this area, you might see or hear some fast-moving planes overhead on their way to Wright-Patterson Air Force Base. Just prior to mile marker 6, you will cross Jacoby Road at-grade, one of the more dangerous crossings because the cars often come quickly around a bend.

The next two miles are peaceful and green. The trail has an almost imperceptible uphill grade along this section, as you begin your approach into Yellow Springs. Near mile marker 8, you will cross under Hyde Road. The bridge above the trail is a popular spot to take "aerial" shots of the trail. At 8.2 you will pass an equestrian center, where trail parking is not allowed.

You will pass the Glen Helen Nature Preserve on the right side near mile marker 9. Here, you can enjoy several hiking trails, a natural area and a trailside museum, although bikes are not allowed. At this point, you will start to notice some campus buildings, which are part of Antioch College, off to the left side. Near 9.3, an entrepreneur has set up an in-line skate and bike rental shop inside a remodeled caboose.

Yellow Springs is a quaint town, ideal for pedestrians. Plan to spend some time strolling in and out of the varied, independently-owned shops. As you cross U.S. Route 68, you will see several eateries and the town's main thoroughfare.

If you continue on the trail, you will soon pass the Bryan Community Center, which includes a large parking lot and restrooms. The trail ends somewhat abruptly at Yellow Springs-Fairfield Road, although an extension to Springfield is in the works.

Little Miami State Park

Endpoints: Kroger Hill to Spring Valley

Location: Hamilton, Clermont, Warren and Greene Counties

Length: 50 miles

Surface: Asphalt (with a parallel dirt shoulder) for 22.5 miles between Milford and Morrow; extremely large, chunky ballast on remaining sections. Entire trail slated to be paved the end of 1995.

Uses: 🚶 🚴 🏇 🎣 🚣

🚲 ♿ 🛼 on certain sections

Contact: Chuck Thiemann, Manager
Little Miami State Park
8570 East State Route 73
Waynesville, OH 45068
513-897-3055

◆◆◆

You won't find any pink flamingos or high-rise beachfront hotels near this trail. This is the *other* Miami—the Little Miami Valley in southwestern Ohio, where a scenic river and a multi-use trail join together to meet just about everybody's recreational needs.

The history of the trail along the Little Miami River dates back to well before the Little Miami Railroad was chartered in 1836. Several native American tribes made their homes along the river, including the Hopewell Indians who lived in the area from 300 B.C to 600 A.D. More recently, members of the Miami and Shawnee

LITTLE MIAMI STATE PARK

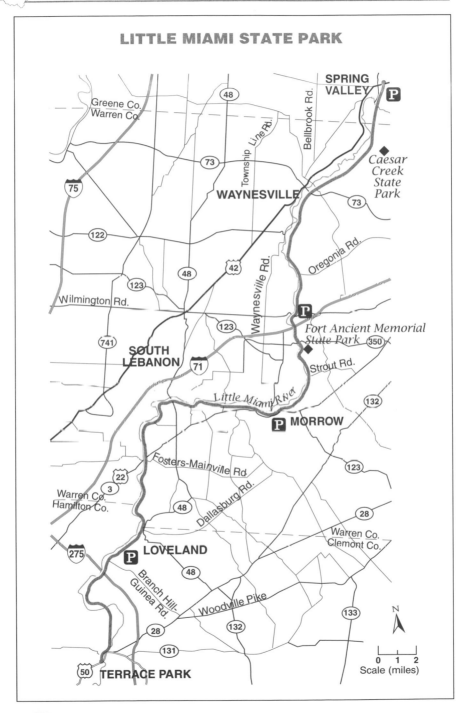

tribes lived in the area and some of their burial mounds are still visible.

By the mid-1800s, the river bustled with grist mills and textile mills, which were serviced by the railroad. During the Civil War, ammunition was transported on the line, which the Pennsylvania Railroad purchased in 1869. The Ohio Department of Natural Resources bought the corridor from the bankrupt Penn Central Corporation in 1979.

Because of fierce local opposition at the trail's southern end, the State Department of Natural Resources developed the 14 miles between Loveland and Morrow in 1984, followed by a 9.5-mile southern extension into Milford in 1991.

The trail's southern two miles are still not developed, although they are slated for completion by September, 1995. Therefore, no southern trailhead currently exists and parking in Milford is practically non-existent. The trail management suggests parking in Loveland, which is not very conducive to seeing the trail's first eight miles. As the trail continues its development in 1995, a new trailhead could be developed.

The paved portion of trail currently begins just west of the Little Miami River near the intersection of State Route 126 and U.S. Route 50. For the first few miles outside of Milford, the trail is fairly wooded and runs parallel to State Route 126 (Glendale-Milford Road). Through the trees you can see the rolling hills and distant farmland. At the two-mile mark, you will find a restaurant and general store that have fairly limited hours. If open, they are one of the few places to stop before the town of Loveland.

Prior to mile marker 3, you cross the rippling Little Miami River, designated a national and state scenic river, for the first time. Then the trail promptly becomes wooded again. You will cross over Route 126, which cuts through the town of Miamiville, where bike rentals are available. The local fire station offers portable toilets, a public telephone and several parking spaces at the corner of Front Street and Perry Lane.

Woodlands and wildflowers surround the trail for the next couple of miles, and just beyond mile marker 5 some river views make a brief return. Within another half-mile, you will cross under Interstate 275. Prior to mile marker 7, you will see an original stone mile marker that reads "C 99," the distance to Columbus.

By mile marker 8, the trail is completely tunneled by trees, including occasional sycamores and hemlocks. When the vegetation starts to subside, it signals your approach into the trail-happy town of Loveland. The trail has sparked significant economic development in the quaint downtown area, where you will find numerous restaurants (most with bike racks), shops, canoe and bike rental outfitters, a refurbished depot and scores of parking spaces. An art gallery, which has sponsored two "Bicycles in Art" exhibits, has even opened in a refurbished, trailside building. To get to downtown Loveland by car, take the Loveland Road exit northeast nearly four miles from Interstate 275.

The Little Miami State Park constantly hosts a mix of trail users.

Soon after the trail crosses Loveland Road, you will arrive at Nisbit Park. With an amphitheater, picnic tables, restrooms, drinking fountains, another sizeable parking lot (including horse trailer spaces), the park demonstrates Loveland's commitment to the trail.

As you leave Loveland by mile marker 9, you head back into forested terrain for the next several miles, and begin a gradual ascent. Between two at-grade crossings, the river makes sporadic appearances on the trail's left side.

At mile marker 15, south of Kings Island, you will see an old industrial structure that currently houses a small bike rental operation. The building dates back at least to the Civil War, when ammunition production began here. When that subsided after World War II, Columbia Records took over the building for several years. The current owner is trying to attract new businesses, and the bike shop rental was an obvious first tenant.

You will skirt the town of South Lebanon near mile marker 17. The next few miles offer excellent birdwatching opportunities, with colorful finches and cardinals fluttering alongside the trail. With any luck, you might spot one of the great blue herons that also reside along the trail. The area remains definitively rural until you reach Morrow.

The developed portion of the trail currently ends approximately 22.5 miles north of Milford in the sleepy town of Morrow. The trailhead includes a small playground, a gazebo, a picnic shelter, ample parking and restrooms. The trailhead is located on Center Street, one block off of U.S. Route 22/State Route 3, about a half mile west of State Route 123.

To continue north on the trail toward Fort Ancient and Spring Valley, you will need a mountain bike, a horse or a sturdy pair of hiking boots. A sense of rugged adventure will also help you conquer the surface—at least until the trail is paved. The state plans to pave this northern section of trail during 1995, so call the manager for the latest developments.

You will travel on-road for a short distance through Morrow. A grey railroad depot with a few vending machines will be on your right. The small restaurant and ice cream shop across the street represent most of the available trailside services for the next 15 miles.

You will cross over a large railroad trestle before venturing into dense woods on your northward journey. For the next couple of miles the trail alternates between densely enclosed hardwood forest and open landscape with occasional glimpses of the Little Miami River.

About three miles from Morrow, the trail runs close to the river, offering exceptional views. In another two miles, you will pass a trail on the right that leads up to the north overlook of Fort Ancient. The climb out of the river valley is steep, but if you are interested in native American sites, including burial mounds, it will be worth the journey.

The area surrounding the trail gets progressively more gorge-like, with side slopes rising on the right and rolling hills taking on more mountainous qualities. Fortunately, the river and the railroad have carved a path through these ridges, not over them.

In another mile, you will see an access area for Fort Ancient State Memorial, dedicated to the native Americans who once inhabited the Little Miami Valley. A large canoe livery operates in the same area, offering trips ranging from two hours to two days. The livery, which is open April-October, also offers inner tubes and riverside camping, not to mention some of the best river views you'll see all day. Take some time to wander down to the river and look around.

Within a mile you will cross under Interstate 71, which has the highest bridge span in Ohio. It will give you a fresh perspective of the gorge through which you are traveling. A little more than seven miles north of Morrow, you will cross through an area known as Mathers Mill, a popular canoeing area. Parking is available adjacent to the trail.

After you cross Wilmington Road, you may notice that the trail surface is even more rugged than before. Depending on your tolerance for getting jostled, you may opt to use Corwin Road, which at this point is to your right. This lightly-traveled road crosses the trail a couple of times, but the two remain basically parallel all the way to Corwin eight miles away.

For the next several miles, the trail is shrouded by trees and seldom changes. The river, while not far away, is virtually out of sight for the remainder of the trail. In about five miles, the trail skirts the edge of Caesar Creek State Nature Preserve, where you

can explore several trails. A parking lot, where restrooms are located, indicates the Preserve. Almost immediately after this lot, you will encounter a short, undeveloped bridge that will force you to use Corwin Road if you aren't already using it.

Karen-Lee Ryan

This railroad trestle in Morrow signals the trail's halfway mark.

Karen-Lee Ryan

The northern end of the Little Miami State Park cuts through rolling farmland.

A crossing under State Route 73 signals your approach into Corwin. You may opt to stay on-road through Corwin, where the trail is basically a green swath between two roads. The town's ice cream shop/restaurant/deli is the only place to get food and beverages until Spring Valley.

For nearly two miles north of Corwin, the surface is thick, chunky ballast. You may want to take New Burlington Road, which parallels the trail's left side for a little more than 1.5 miles. But, be sure to get back onto the trail where the road crosses the corridor. After the trail veers away from the road, you will travel through an open area with graceful rolling hills in the distance.

Beyond this point, the trail is again enclosed by trees, basically turning into a bumpy two-track. Soon after crossing into Greene County, the trail passes through the Spring Valley Wildlife Area, where wildflowers abound and hunting is allowed between September and January. The remaining three miles to Spring Valley are rugged and overgrown, with the trail becoming just a single track amid thick vegetation.

Wilma Frey

Wild phlox thrives along the Little Miami State Park.

Less than two miles south of the town of Spring Valley, you will cross Roxanna-New Burlington Road at-grade, followed closely by an industrial plant that appears to use the trail as a driveway and loading dock. The trail cuts through the edge of Spring Valley between Bank and Elm Streets. Parking is available about a block and a half from the trail at Walton Park, where swing sets, picnic tables, baseball diamonds and portable toilets are available.

The state of Ohio owns the trail for another three miles, although it will not be developed until late 1995. The corridor continues under Greene County ownership and is still in the planning and design phases.

Within a couple of years, the Little Miami State Park will connect directly to Greene County's Little Miami Scenic Trail, currently open between Xenia and Yellow Springs (see page 241). Future plans call for extending the trail north all the way Springfield. And, on the southern end, the trail may one day continue to the Ohio Riverfront, creating an 80-mile contiguous route from downtown Cincinnati to Springfield.

Olentangy-Scioto Bikeway

Endpoints: Columbus to Worthington

Location: Franklin County

Length: 1.5 miles of an 18-mile trail on an abandoned rail line

Surface: Asphalt, concrete

Uses:

Contact: Mollie O'Donnell, Landscape Architect
City of Columbus Recreation and Parks Department
420 W. Whittier Street
Columbus, OH 43215
614-645-3300

◆◆◆

The Olentangy-Scioto Bikeway epitomizes the urban trail. Making use of rail and river corridors, as well as streets through Columbus, the Olentangy-Scioto Bikeway traverses varied terrain and connects suburban areas with small city parks and downtown Columbus.

Built in 1969, this rail-trail and bike path were Ohio's first. Since the trail was not built to today's engineering standards, some sections have sharp curves and narrow bridges and sidewalks. However, if you use caution, the Olentangy-Scioto Bikeway offers a unique and largely unseen view of the greater Columbus area.

The trail can be divided into three parts. The older five-mile southern section parallels the Scioto River and connects downtown Columbus to its waterfront parks. The fragmented mid-section consists of short strips of riverfront trail interspersed with

OLENTANGY-SCIOTO BIKEWAY

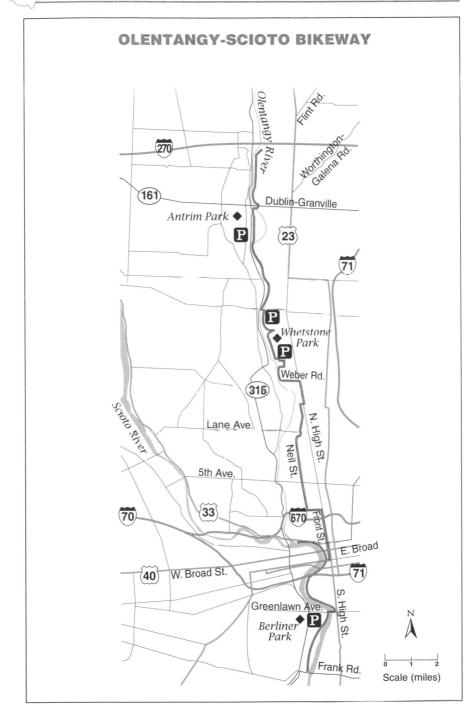

Shawn Richardson

You can view the attractive Columbus skyline from the Olentangy-Scioto Bikeway.

connecting streets. And, the continuous eight-mile northern section follows the Olentangy River and travels through suburban communities with wooded areas and several spacious parks. There are no mileage markers along the trail.

The southern trailhead is located at Lou Berliner Park. From Interstate 70, take Interstate 71 south to the Greenlawn Avenue exit. Turn right on Deckebach Road, which is the park's entrance. Turn left on Stimmel, and the trail will parallel your left side. While the trail is not marked with signs, you will see its tree-lined edge. You can park behind the sports complex.

The trail actually begins at Frank Road, a half-mile south of the park. Currently, no trail access exists at the southern terminus. However, it is worth exploring this small section of trail, formerly a rail corridor. It travels through a canopy of trees above the west bank and flood plains of the Scioto River. At Greenlawn Avenue, 1.5 miles from Frank Road, the path (and former rail line) end. Pass under the Greenlawn Avenue bridge on a steep down and up incline and continue on the opposite (east) side of the river. Using city sidewalks, follow bike route signs and the river. A small parking lot is available along Front Street near Greenlawn Avenue.

At mile two you enter the western edge of German Village, a unique residential and commercial historic district filled with brick sidewalks, parks and small brick homes. If you want to explore the area, turn right on Whittier Street. To continue on the bike route, turn left on Whittier and cross over the bridge. You will see a sign ahead that reads "Lower Scioto Bikeway," indicating the reappearance of the asphalt trail. Downhill and off to the left, you will see a small parking lot and boat ramp.

Traveling through a wooded area along the Scioto river, this mile of the trail attracts many lunch-time joggers from downtown Columbus. About 3.3 miles from Frank Road, you will pass under Interstate 70 and a railroad trestle. Next, you will be up on a stone sidewalk with white pipe railings. Over the rushing waters of a dam, the skyscrapers of downtown Columbus rise up, offering a post-card view of the city.

Before mile four, the trail crosses Main Street and leads into Bicentennial Park, where you will find picnic tables and benches. From here, you can connect to the Olentangy Bikeway via city streets or continue for another mile on the Scioto Bike Path, where you will pass through another park and see nice views of downtown Columbus and the confluence of the Olentangy and Scioto Rivers.

Shawn Richardson

The southern portion of the trail is developed on a former rail line.

To stay on the trail, follow the sidewalk along the river adjacent to Civic Center Drive. At mile 4.25 you enter Battelle Riverfront Park, where a replica of Christopher Columbus' Santa Maria floats dockside. You can tour the boat between May and December. You can also rent paddleboats in warm weather. Picnic tables, bike racks and a water fountain are also available at this small, attractive park near the heart of downtown. City Center (a large enclosed shopping plaza), restaurants and the State Capitol are within a few blocks. The trail resumes briefly beyond the park, heading north along the river.

The trail passes under another railroad trestle and ends abruptly along Spring Street (U.S. 33), beneath the State Route 315 overpass. The Columbus Parks and Recreation Department plans to continue the trail northward in the near future. Call the trail manager for current information.

To reach the northern section of the Olentangy-Scioto Bikeway, you must make unsigned street connections in downtown Columbus. If you travel this way on bike, use caution on the busy streets. From the Bicentennial Park area, travel east on Rich Street and then north onto one-way Front Street for a mile. When you cross a set of railroad tracks, you are entering an area called the Short North. If you are hungry, turn right on Spruce Street and visit the indoor North Market.

Continue straight on Front Street/Park Avenue, where you will pass Goodale Park. Turn left on Buttles Avenue, and make a right onto Neil Avenue. Travel three-quarters of a mile through Victorian Village and then straight through the Ohio State University campus on Neil Avenue. At Dodridge Avenue, turn east and go one block to High Street, a very busy thoroughfare.

Continue north on High Street and turn west on Weber. When the street ends, the Olentangy-Scioto Bikeway resumes. The trail follows the river for a half mile behind the residential area of Clintonville and then ends at Delhi Avenue. From here you travel on-street following bike route signs for another half-mile.

The northern third of the Olentangy-Scioto Bikeway resumes at the end of Northmoor Place Road, where there is a small parking lot. The trail takes on its now familiar feel with an expanse of park on the left and the river beyond. The trail leads into woods for a half-mile, then curves to the right and enters Whetstone Park. The

Whetstone Park trailhead is also a popular place to begin the trail. Picnic facilities, restrooms and parking are available. The Park of Roses, at the eastern end, offers a beautiful and extensive rose and herb garden.

In the next mile, you will pass a reflecting pool, athletic fields and a pedestrian bridge. The trail rises to Henderson Road where cyclists are requested to walk their bikes as they turn left across the bridge. Passing under the bridge, the trail hugs the river bank on the right. Proceed through a country-like stretch of trees and brush and then continue into denser woods for about a half-mile. You will cross several small, wooden bridges. The woods thin out, and the river is visible intermittently on the right.

Soon the trail enters Antrim Park, probably the most idyllic and heavily used spot on the trail. Here a wooded area separates the trail from the highway as the trail skirts Antrim Lake on its west side. A third lane for pedestrians has been added. Bicycles are prohibited on the other three sides of the lake.

Antrim Park is a popular place for a stroll or skate around the lake. People also fish from the banks or just stop to enjoy the view. A parking lot and toilets are available west of the trail under the 315 overpass. Access to the park by car is from Olentangy River Road. Past Antrim Park, the trail veers to the left again paralleling Highway 315.

Follow the signs over and under the State Route 161 bridge. The rather narrow trail now curves and meanders through a thickly wooded, scenic area. The trail meets the Olentangy Parkland Fitness Trail, which has exercise stations at intervals. It is possible to continue straight through, or to take the loop back. Beyond the Fitness Trail, the trail forks. Take the left fork and go over a small wooden bridge. The trail is curvy and narrow in places. The right fork takes you east to an exit on Masefield Street in a residential area of Worthington.

Continuing straight, the trail goes under a highway overpass and curves to the right. You will pass tennis courts on the left where a shelter, picnic table and drinking water are available. The trail then turns left toward Wilson Bridge Road, the trail's northern endpoint. There is a small parking lot here—off Wilson Bridge just east of State Route 315—and a sign indicating the Olentangy Bikeway.

Stavich Bicycle Trail

Endpoints: Struthers, Ohio to New Castle, Pennsylvania

Location: Mahoning County, Ohio, and Lawrence County, Pennsylvania

Length: 10 miles

Surface: Asphalt

Uses:

Contact: Gary Slaven
Falcon Foundry
6th and Water Streets
Lowellville, OH 44436-0301
216-536-6221

◆◆◆

One of the nation's few interstate rail-trails, the Stavich Bicycle Trail parallels the scenic Mahoning River, and offers an intriguing look at the waning steel industry.

In its heyday, the Mahoning Valley boasted nearly a dozen steel mills, with six parallel railroad tracks to serve them. Today, the industry has all but dried up in the area, although many of the buildings remain. Two railroad lines are still active, including the CSX main line that runs adjacent to the Stavich Bicycle Trail.

Interestingly, the trail is actually built on a former interurban electric line that ran between Youngstown, Ohio, and New Castle, Pennsylvania. Interurbans were allowed to have steeper grades than freight railroads, so you'll encounter a few hills on the Stavich. Abandoned in 1933, the line remained largely intact because it paralleled so many active rail lines.

STAVICH BICYCLE TRAIL

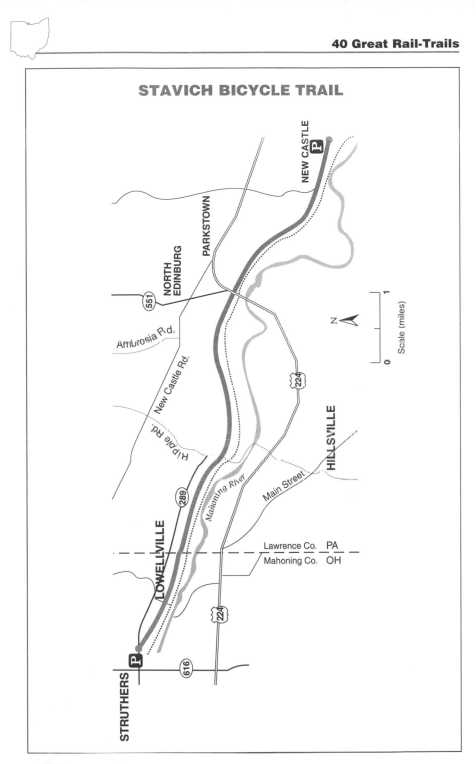

Built in 1983, the Stavich Bicycle Trail resulted from an all-volunteer effort. Donations from the Stavich family and many other local individuals made the trail possible.

The Ohio trailhead is located on State Route 289 about one mile east of State Route 616. It's hard to miss the large, raised sign as you approach the parking lot.

Struthers was once the major railroad switching yard between Cleveland and Pittsburgh. As you begin the trail, you will notice an expansive area between the trail and the Mahoning River. At one time, nearly 20 tracks lined the area.

At the outset, the trail can be a little scruffy, with overgrown vegetation lining the left side. Two active railroad tracks are on your right, although the remnants of many more are still visible. Within a mile, you will pass by the football field of the local high school, and soon you will enter the town of Lowellville. The trail is located on Liberty Street through the town, where you will see City Hall, a post office, a small market and a gazebo. Within a half-mile, the trail again separates from the road and continues its industrial feel.

You will reach the Ohio-Pennsylvania border at the three-mile mark, which is indicated by the trail's first mileage marker. There

David Chappell

Active trains alongside the Stavich Trail remind users of the route's heritage.

is also an old stone "State Line" post with Pennsylvania on one side and Ohio on the other.

In a short distance, you will be making a fairly steep, although short, ascent. When you get to the top just beyond the 3.5-mile mark, take a moment to look around. You get the best views of the Mahoning River from this high point, where it is also easy to envision all the steam engines that once passed below. If you wait long enough, you may even see an active railroad chug by.

By mile marker 5, you will have come all the way back down the hill, and, if it's late summer or early fall, goldenrod (which is mixed with daisies and sumac further up the trail) may be engulfing you from both sides of the trail. The tone of the trail seems to shift from industrial to more pastoral at this point, where you can see farmland in the background. At the same time, an embankment rises briefly on the left, giving the trail a faraway feeling.

The thick vegetation over the next few miles attracts small mammals such as woodchucks. You may also see a variety of birds, including red-tail hawks, woodpeckers and numerous colorful finches.

Near the 7.5-mile mark, you will cross under U.S. Route 224, and as you approach mile marker 8, you will pass some interesting wetlands on the trail's left side.

When you have gone more than 9.5 miles from Struthers, you will see the parking area at the New Castle end of the trail. The trail continues past the parking lot approximately 0.3 miles before ending at Covert Road. Union Township recently received funding to build a rest stop and river overlook near the trail's eastern end. The project will increase the parking in this area and offer another opportunity to view the Mahoning River Valley.

Thomas J. Evans Bike Trail

Endpoints: Johnstown to Newark

Location: Licking County

Length: 14.5 miles

Surface: Asphalt

Uses: 🚶 🚲 ♿ 🛼 🎣 ⛷️

Contact: The Thomas J. Evans Foundation
P.O. Box 4212
Newark, OH 43055
614-345-9711

Licking Park District
4309 Lancaster Road
Granville, OH 43023
614-587-2535

◆◆◆

Thomas J. Evans was a pharmacist from Licking County, who made wise investments during his life. Before he died, he set up a foundation to create educational and recreational opportunities for the citizens of Licking County. The foundation funded the popular Thomas J. Evans Bike Trail.

The corridor that is now the trail began as the Toledo and Ohio Central Railroad. Built in 1877, the route's primary purpose was to transport coal between the Ohio River Valley and the Toledo area, although it also served as a passenger route. In the 1930s, New York Central purchased the line, which became a Penn Central route during the 1960s—only to be abandoned in 1970. The Thomas J. Evans Foundation funded the trail, which opened in 1983, and continues to maintain it today.

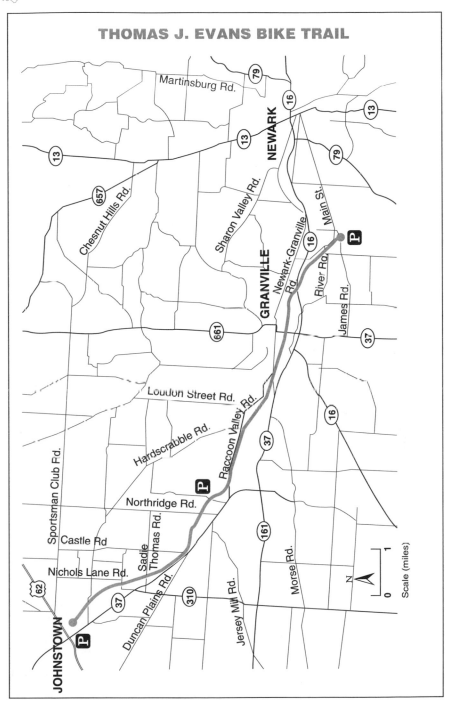

THOMAS J. EVANS BIKE TRAIL

The trailhead in Johnstown is located just southeast of U.S. Route 62 and State Route 37. Take Douglas Avenue east from Route 37 to the parking lot, which abuts an area that looks like a truck parking area. The parking lot is not representative of the rest of the trail.

As soon as you embark on the trail, you will be cutting through rolling farmland, typical scenery for central Ohio. In less than a mile, you will cut over an active railroad track, so use caution. The mileage markers are painted on the asphalt surface. They start in Newark, so you will pass mile 13 at the one-mile mark if you begin in Johnstown.

Soon you will pass the first of several informational signs along the route. The first one describes the Wyandot tribe of native Americans, who settled in the area known today as Licking County. Within two miles of the Johnstown trailhead, the trail gets more wooded, with occasional residences dotting the surrounding area. The asphalt surface shows its age in several places, although it has been sporadically patched.

Beyond mile four, the trail gets progressively more rural, with corn growing up to the edge of the trail by mid-summer. The trail's

Richard H. Mueller

Wildwood Park offers a playful diversion from the Evans Trail.

Linda Hanlon

The Evans Trail is a great place to take a stroll.

first bench is located near the 4.5-mile mark, and another interesting sign appears at mile six. A portable toilet is also located here. Several houses are scattered along the trail's left side for the next mile, while corn continues to line the right side.

Before the 8.5-mile mark, you will be passing an area that was once the town of Clemons, where up to 15 trains a day picked up fuel, water and passengers in the late 1800s. The railroad station also doubled as a 24-hour telegraph office. Today, an interpretive marker along the trail tells the story of this former town.

The Raccoon River parallels the trail's eastern end, and you will begin picking up views of it around the nine-mile mark. In less than a mile, you will cross Old Route 37 at grade before returning to the wooded corridor. Family-oriented Wildwood Park, where you will find a large playground, picnic tables, soccer fields, portable toilets and parking, offers a pleasant green setting near the 10.5-mile mark.

As you head toward Granville, you will notice some new development along the trail near mile marker 11. Next, you will pass the restored red and white Granville train station that now houses a real estate office. You will cross busy State Route 661, which leads directly into Granville. Dennison University is located here, and you will find several restaurants, banks and shops in the quaint downtown area.

After the road crossing, you will briefly cut behind a small industrial area and water treatment plant. Soon, you will return to the peaceful trail paralleling Raccoon Creek, where you might see a beaver, some turtles or a great blue heron. The landscape surrounding the trail becomes a mix of farmland and homes as you near the city of Newark.

About 1.5 miles from the eastern endpoint, you will cross over an original railroad trestle, where another signs explains the route's history. As you continue toward Newark, a steep embankment lines the trail's right side. In the summer, wildflowers flourish on either side of the trail. The rippling river, below the trail and to your left, adds to the striking scenery of this area.

Just before the trail ends in the western side of Newark, where plenty of parking is available, you will pass a trail kiosk that includes information on the founder of the Evans Foundation. This seems a fitting ending to one of the nation's few rail-trails managed by a private foundation.

Karen-Lee Ryan

A portion of the Wolf Creek Bikeway cuts through Sycamore State Park.

Wolf Creek Bikeway

Endpoints: Trotwood to Brookville

Location: Montgomery County

Length: 11 miles (will be 13 when completed)

Surface: Hard-packed crushed limestone

Uses: 🚶 🚲

Contact: Dayton-Montgomery County Park District
1375 East Siebenthaler Avenue
Dayton, OH 45414-5398
513-278-8231

◆◆◆

Cooperation has been the key word in getting the Wolf Creek Bikeway built. Working together, the Dayton-Montgomery Park District, the towns of Trotwood and Brookville and the townships of Madison and Perry built the first 11 miles of the Wolf Creek Bikeway. Each entity provided personnel or equipment or assisted with development costs. The result is an attractive rail-trail that connects several communities and a state park.

The corridor was originally developed by the Greenville and Miami Railroad Company in 1852. When this company foreclosed the line in 1861, the Dayton and Miami Railroad took control of it. Over the years, the line went through eight different mergers until it was abandoned in 1992.

The City of Trotwood, the Village of Brookville and the Dayton-Montgomery Park District purchased the right of way upon the line's abandonment. Other agencies soon joined to help develop the trail, which went from abandonment to completed trail in record time.

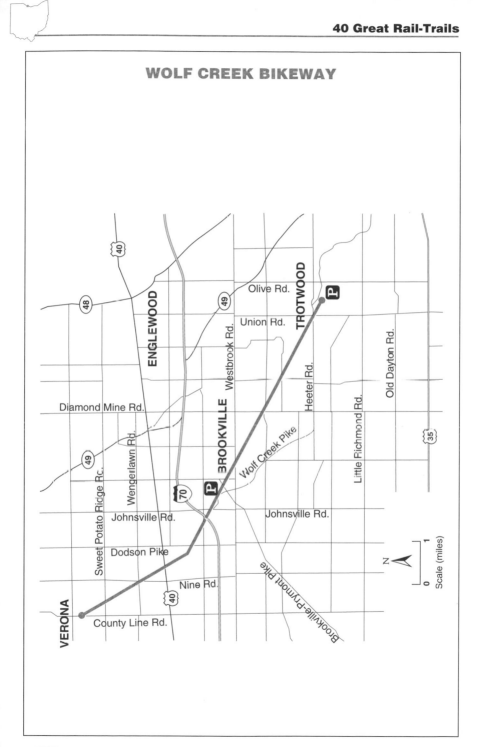

WOLF CREEK BIKEWAY

The trail begins in downtown Trotwood, about 10 miles northwest of Dayton. A blue B&O Caboose and restored depot are part of the Old Town Commons at Main and Broadway. To get there, take Union Road four miles north from U.S. Route 35 to the town of Trotwood, where you will head east on Main Street for less than a block. Parking is adjacent to the depot, which is managed by the local historical society.

The developed portion of the trail, which officially opened in spring 1994, heads directly northwest. The abandoned corridor continues southeast, and future plans call for extending it all the way into Dayton, where it will connect with existing bikeways along the Great Miami River.

The trail initially cuts behind a residential area, and within a half-mile, the trail parallels Sycamore State Park on the left. This 2,368-acre park offers numerous trails for equestrians and hikers, as well as a cross-country skiing trail and a snowmobiling trail. A picnic area and shelters are also available at the park, which is in the process of developing a new parking lot to service the trail.

The trail has a minimal uphill grade for its entire length, and the next couple of miles get progressively more rural. The park continues to line the trail's left side, offering hundreds of wildflowers and attractive grasslands to the otherwise flat, yet attractive, surroundings.

Beyond the three-mile mark, you will cross Shiloh Springs Road at grade, followed soon by Diamond Mine Road. Just beyond this road, the surface becomes noticeably more hard-packed and smooth. Power lines also appear, towering above this open trail. In the summer, you can get very hot while traveling the route because there are no trees to provide shade. But thanks to the patches of wildflowers that attract butterflies and birds, the trail is pleasantly scenic.

The next major at-grade crossing is Heckathorn Road. About 5.5 miles from Trotwood, you will see a few industrial buildings amid some private residences adjacent to the trail. Because this trail was converted soon after its abandonment, many of the railroad relics are still in place along the line, including switchboxes and whistleposts.

In another half-mile, you will enter Brookville, where the historical society maintains a depot and a caboose. An original rail-

road crossing sign also has been preserved. In town, you can find some eateries and a couple of small shops.

At this point, you can probably see Interstate 70 in the distance ahead of you. Before getting there, however, you will pass Golden Gate Park on your right. Here you will find a running track, several baseball fields, a basketball court, portable toilets and plenty of parking. The trail crosses Arlington Road at-grade, where you will find a smattering of fast-food restaurants primarily supported by Interstate 70.

The trail crosses under the highway and ends about 1.5 miles south of Verona, located at the Montgomery County line. The abandoned corridor actually continues all the way to Indiana, but it is unclear whether or not it will be developed beyond the Montgomery County line.

Saturn Retailer Locations

For more information, please call 1-800-522-5000.

PENNSYLVANIA

Saturn of Carlisle Pike
6515 Carlisle Pike
Mechanicsburg, PA 17055
717-796-1111

Saturn of Doylestown
Route 313 & 611 Bypass
Doylestown, PA 18901
215-348-5990

Saturn of Harrisburg
1301 Paxton Street
Harrisburg, PA 17104
717-234-8888

Saturn of Jenkintown
1760 The Fairway
Jenkintown, PA 19046
215-884-7140

Saturn of Lancaster
1530 Manheim Pike
Lancaster, PA 17601
717-560-5777

Saturn of Reading
2526 Centre Avenue
Reading, PA 19605
610-921-1314

Saturn of The Valley
501-23 State Road
Emmaus, PA 18049
610-965-5400

Saturn of Trevose
4437 Street Road
Trevose, PA 19503
215-364-3980

Saturn of West Chester
700 West Town Road
West Chester, PA 19382
610-429-3100

Saturn of Wyoming Valley
2140 San Souci Parkway
Hanover Township, PA 18702
717-823-6555

Saturn of York
951 North Hills Road
York, PA 17402
717-757-3383

Saturn of Monroeville
4200 William Penn Highway
Monroeville, PA 15146
412-372-8876

Saturn of West Liberty
2855 West Liberty Avenue
Dormont, PA 15216
412-572-7000

Saturn of Wexford
10247 Perry Highway
Wexford, PA 15090
412-935-6677

NEW JERSEY

Saturn of Bordentown
237 Route 130
Bordentown, NJ 08505
609-291-1000

Saturn of Brunswick
1500 US Route 1
North Brunswick, NJ 08902
908-418-1888

Saturn of Denville
3103 Route 10 East
Denville, NJ 07834
201-361-0400

Saturn of Eatontown
67 Highway 36
Eatontown, NJ 07724
908-389-8822

Saturn of Englewood
105 Grand Avenue
Englewood, NJ 07631
201-567-5353

Saturn of Freehold
4039 Route 9 North
Freehold, NJ 07728
908 303-8700

Saturn of Jersey City
943 Communipaw Avenue
Jersey City, NJ 07304
201-433-2121

Saturn of Livingston
On the Route 10/Livingston Circle
Livingston, NJ 07309
201-992-0600

Saturn of Morristown
50 Morris Street
Morristown, NJ 07960
201-538-2800

Saturn of Mt. Laurel
1311 Route 73
Mt. Laurel, NJ 08054
609-778-3000

Saturn of Ramsey
815 Route 17 South
Ramsey, NJ 07446
201-327-2500

Saturn of Route 23
561 Route 23 South
Pompton Plains, NJ 07444
201-839-2222

Saturn of Toms River
1199 Route 37 East
Toms River, NJ 08753
908-506-0500

Saturn of Turnersville
160 South Blackhorse Pike
Turnsville, NJ 08012
609-728-1500

Saturn of Union
2675 Route 22 West
Union, NJ 07083
908-686-2810

MARYLAND

Saturn of Bel Air
716 Bel Air Road
Bel Air, MD 21014
410-879-2600

Saturn of Ellicott City
8431 Baltimore National Pike Blvd.
Ellicott City, MD 21043
410-313-9000

Saturn of Frederick
5903 Urbana Pike
Frederick, MD 21701
301-663-1300

Saturn of Gaithersburg
16160 Frederick Road
Gaithersburg, MD 20898
301-948-4100

Saturn of Glen Burnie
12 Holsum Way
Glen Burnie, MD 21061
410-760-3000

Saturn of Marlow Heights
4601 St. Barnabas Road
Marlow Heights, MD 20748
301-423-3111

Saturn of Owings Mills
11216 Reistertown Road
Owings Mills, MD 21117
410-356-1861

Saturn of York Road
1630 York Road
Lutherville, MD 21093
410-494-2500

VIRGINIA

Saturn of Alexandria
1525 Kenwood Avenue
Alexandria, VA 22302
703-998-5600

Saturn of Fairfax
9596 Old Lee Highway
Fairfax, VA 22031
703-359-8080

Saturn of Fredericksburg
3421 Jefferson Davis Highway
Fredericksburg, VA 22401
703-373-7100

Saturn of Newport News
12602 Jefferson Avenue
Newport News, VA 23602
804-872-0512

Saturn of Richmond
11840 Midlothian Turnpike
Midlothian, VA 23113
804-379-9922

Saturn of Roanoke Valley
1022 East Main Street
Salem, VA 24153
703-389-1214

Saturn of Sterling
46980 Harry Byrd Highway
Sterling, VA 22170
703-389-1214

Saturn of Virginia Beach
1808 Lasking Road
Virginia Beach, VA 23454
804-422-2099

Saturn West Broad
8066 West Broad Street
Richmond, VA 23294
804-747-4090

Saturn of Woodbridge
14211 Jefferson Davis Highway
Woodbridge, VA 22191
703-643-0999

WEST VIRGINIA

Saturn of Clarksburg
Route 19 South
Clarksburg, WV 26301
304-624-6012

Saturn of Charleston/Huntington
One Saturn Way
Hurricane, WV 25526
304-562-3300

OHIO

Saturn of Dayton
995 Miamisburg-Centerville Road
Dayton, OH 45459
513-436-0098

Saturn of Chapel Hill
247 Howe Avenue
Cuyahoga Falls, OH 44221
216-923-8000

Saturn of Kings Auto Mall
9536 Kings Auto Mall Road
Cincinnati, OH 45249
513-583-9300

Saturn of Mansfield
1400 Park Avenue West
Mansfield, OH 44906
419-529-7500

Saturn/North
8600 North High Street
Worthington, OH 43085
614-436-2001

Saturn of Route 422
420 Youngstown-Warren Road
Niles, OH 44446
216-544-2000

Saturn of Springdale
95 West Kemper Road
Springdale, OH 45246
513-782-2800

Saturn of Sunnyside
7629 Pearl Road
Middleburg Heights, OH 44130
216-243-7711

Saturn of Toledo
5551 West Central Avenue
Toledo, OH 43615
419-531-5175

Saturn/West
3880 Fishinger Boulevard
Hilliard, OH 43026
614-771-9700

Saturn of Wickliffe
28840 Euclid Avenue
Wickliffe, OH 44092
216-585-1000

Saturn of Beechmont
8021 Beechmont Avenue
Cincinnati, OH 45255
513-474-5600

Saturn of North Olmsted
2700 Lorain Road
North Olmsted, OH 44070
216-777-8883

Saturn of Mentor
6930 Center Boulevard
Mentor, OH 44060

How to Become a Rails-to-Trails Conservancy Member

RAILS -to- **TRAILS** CONSERVANCY

Rails-to-Trails Conservancy is a private, non-profit public charity, supported by the generous contributions of its members and friends —individuals and families like you. We invite you to join today.

Membership/Gift Membership Levels

Individual Membership **$18**

Supporting Membership **$25**

Patron Membership **$50**

Benefactor Membership **$100**

Advocate Membership **$500**

Trailblazer Society Membership **$1,000**

As a member of Rails-to-Trails Conservancy, you will receive the following benefits:

◆ A free subscription to our quarterly newsletter **Trailblazer.**

◆ A free copy of the **Sampler of America's Rail-Trails**.

◆ Discounts on Conservancy publications, merchandise and conferences.

◆ Additional membership benefits for Trailblazer Society members.

And, most importantly, you will get the satisfaction that comes from helping build a nationwide network of beautiful trails for all of us to enjoy for years (and generations) to come.

Why don't you become an RTC member today?
(Use the order form on page 281)

Rails-to-Trails Conservancy
Merchandise and Publications

RAILS
- to -
TRAILS
CONSERVANCY

40 Great Rail-Trails in Michigan, Illinois, and Indiana
RTC's first in a series of eight regional guides! This 224-page guide book is complete with detailed maps, photographs, and descriptions of 40 of the best rail-trails in the Midwest. Size 5½ x 8½ inches. 1994. **#RG1** $14.95 (Members $12.95).

Pennsylvania's Rail-Trails
This 4 x 9 inch guide fits in your pocket for easy access to detailed maps, trail highlights, and historical background on Pennsylvania's 60 rail-trails. This book covers more than 700 miles of trails throughout the Keystone State. 105 pp. 1994. **#PTG** $12.95. (Members $19.95).

500 Great Rail-Trails
Our most popular publication! This directory offers information such as location, endpoints, length, surface material, contacts and allowable uses for 500 rail-trails in 44 states. **500 Great Rail-Trails #GRT** $9.95 (Members $7.95)

RTC short-sleeve T-Shirt
Printed on 100% cotton, this six-panel T-shirt tells the Rails-to-Trails story in a colorful design. Made in U.S.A.. Indicate size on the order form: S, M, L, X-L). **#TSS** $16.95 (Members $12.95)

RTC Water Bottle
Quench your thirst with this six-panel design water bottle! This colorful, heavy-duty water bottle holds 28 ounces and the exciting colors match the RTC t-shirt. **#WBBN** $4.95 (Members $3.95)

Secrets of Successful Rail-Trails
If you want to help convert an abandoned corridor into a rail-trail, this book is for you. It offers a step-by-step process for organizing supporters, working with government agencies, getting publicity, finding funds to build a trail and much more! **#SST** $19.95 (Members $16.95)

Contents

Maryland

Virginia

West Virginia

Ohio